BARNABY'S FRIENDS AND FANS HAVE SPOKEN...

"A SERIES OF COMIC STRIPS WHICH, LAID END TO END, REACH FROM HERE TO WHEREVER YOU WANT TO GO JUST ONCE BEFORE YOU DIE."

—*The New York Times*

"I WANT TO RECOMMEND *BARNABY* FOR THE CHRISTMAS STOCKINGS OF ALL PARENTS, UNCLES, AND OTHER ADULTS IN GOOD STANDING." —*Chicago Sunday Tribune*

"THE GREATEST BOOK SINCE *WAR AND PEACE*."

—*J.J. O'Malley*

"CROCKETT JOHNSON'S *BARNABY* COMES AS A BREATH OF SWEET, COOL AIR."

—*Life Magazine*

BARNABY BOOKS
Published by Ballantine Books

#1 WANTED: A FAIRY GODFATHER
#2 MR. O'MALLEY AND THE HAUNTED HOUSE
#3 JACKEEN J. O'MALLEY FOR CONGRESS
#4 MR. O'MALLEY GOES FOR THE GOLD*
#5 MR. O'MALLEY, WIZARD OF WALL STREET*

—AND LOTS MORE TO COME…

*Forthcoming

Jackeen J. O'Malley For Congress

by

CROCKETT JOHNSON

A Del Rey Book
Ballantine Books • New York

A Del Rey Book
Published by Ballantine Books

Library of Congress Catalong Card Number: 85-91212

ISBN 0-345-32981-3

Designed by Gene Siegal

Manufactured in the United States of America

First Ballantine Books Edition: January 1986

A TIME THERE WAS
(and not so long ago)

when the world was very different for a five-year-old boy with an active mind.

There was no *Sesame Street* to immobilize him before a screen where puppets and clowns made games of letters and numbers. There were no Saturday cartoons to stultify his imagination with cliché supermen and wild events unrelated to his experience. Indeed, there was no television to hold him from the activities his mind and body needed to develop his growing abilities fully.

There were stories his parents might tell him or read to him, but those required mental creativity to flesh out the words.

It was a safer time, when a child might be free to explore the local haunted house with delighted shudders or wander into nearby woods to climb trees, chase squirrels, or pretend the shadows hid Indians, dragons, or ogres . . .

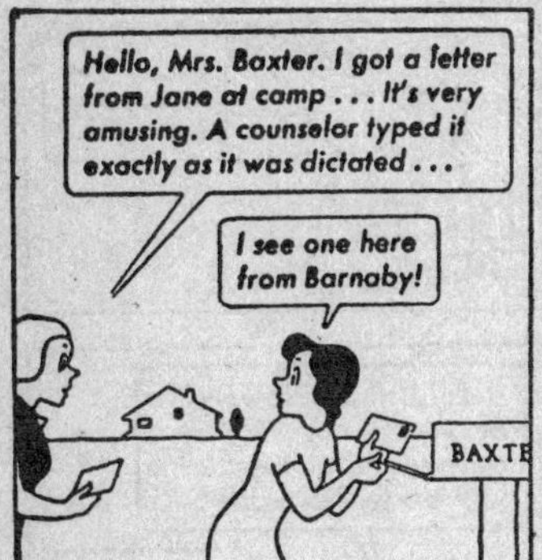
Hello, Mrs. Baxter. I got a letter from Jane at camp . . . It's very amusing. A counselor typed it exactly as it was dictated . . .
I see one here from Barnaby!
BAXTE
8-27

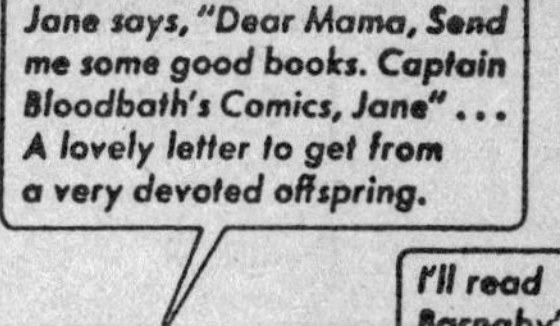
Jane says, "Dear Mama, Send me some good books. Captain Bloodbath's Comics, Jane" . . . A lovely letter to get from a very devoted offspring.

I'll read Barnaby's.

If only he doesn't mention that absurd cigar-smoking little pixie with pink wings. We hope he's getting over imagining—Look at this!

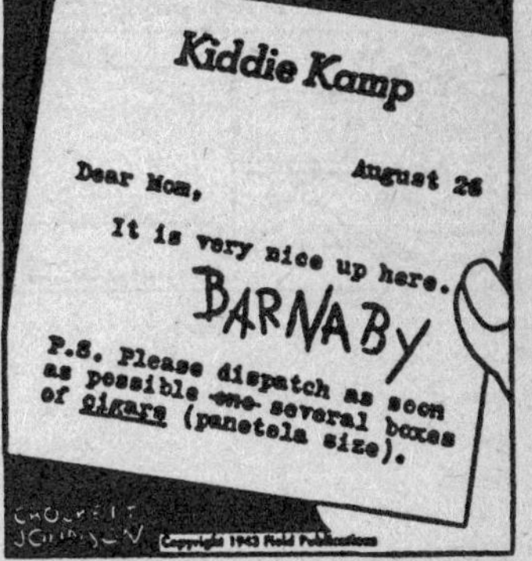
Kiddie Kamp
Dear Mom,
August 26
It is very nice up here.
BARNABY
P.S. Please dispatch as soon as possible ~~one~~ several boxes of cigars (panetela size).
Copyright 1943 Field Publications

Gus and the hermit are still trying to stop the jukebox at Callaghan's . . . I'm commencing to see their point . . . "My Wild Irish Rose" played non-stop for three days palls a bit . . .
8-28
OFFICE
Speaking of entertainment, Barnaby, THIS place could stand some . . . A troupe of those movie starlets. Or a radio show! Bob Hope and Kay Kyser play at camps— Say! Where's a telephone?
But, maybe Mrs. Krump wouldn't—
I see . . . The commercial angle . . . But that's usually obviated by a tautological statement from the sponsor . . . "This broadcast does not constitute an endorsement of our product by Mrs. Krump's Kiddie Kamp as the Kiddie Kamp does not endorse ANY products."
Hello! Hello? Hollywood? Mr. Benny? J. J. O'Malley calling . . . O'Malley . . . the well-known impresario . . .
Doesn't Jack Benny know who you are, Mr. O'Malley?
CROCKET JOHNSO

Hello.
Good morning, little girl.
Hello, Barnaby. . . . I spent the night at Mrs. Krump's phone apprising Hollywood stars of their rôles in my extravaganza.
8 30

But they lacked the enthusiasm I insist upon and I'm recasting the whole show! . . . You, m'boy, get Bob Hope's part. And Jane takes over Hedy Lamarr's lines. . . . Everyone in the Kiddie Kamp displaces a stellar personage!
Gosh!

You may announce this gala spectacle to your assembled playmates in the dining hall. I must find some elephants for the big first act finale. . .
I'll tell everybody right away! . . .

Are you going to tell the children about the little entertainment we want to put on for their parents?
Not before breakfast. . . They'd be so excited they wouldn't eat.
CROCKETT JOHNSON

I've got the six children in the "Ballet of the Bees" rigged out in their muslin wings. They're waiting for you to rehearse them. . . . I believe they expect to be able to fly. . . . They're the most imaginative kids in camp.
I chose them especially. . . . I'm positive they'll become so engrossed in their own wings they'll cease to be impressed by that pixie they all imagine they've seen flying around here. . .
B·31

What's keeping Mrs. Krump?
Hey, Barnaby. . . Here comes your Fairy Godfather.

Barnaby, I've thought of an act that will bolster up the show enormously. My card trick—Say! What are you wearing? Wings!
CROCKETT JOHNSON
Copyright 1943 Field Publications

We're "bees" in the camp show, Mr. O'Malley. . . . These are only make-believe wings we have.
Make-believe? You can see them. . . . And feel them. . . . They're real enough, m'boy.
Barnaby means we can't really fly with them. . .
Nonsense! What are wings for, if not to fly with?
And a woman like Mrs. Krump wouldn't issue apparatus of an inferior quality. . . . There'd be a scandal. . . . Investigations—No! These must be first-class wings. . . . I'm sure they've been load tested and inspected. . . .
Gee!
Copyright 1943 Field Publications
You can't take off by jumping up in the air like that. You're not helicopters. . . You need a long flat runway—I have it!
But—
That dock out over the lake!
CROCKETT JOHNSON

But, Mr. O'Malley. . . We're not supposed to fly. We're "bees" and we run around sniffing other kids in the show who are supposed to be flowers.
Oh, boy.
I understand, m'boy. But this will add an extra punch to the number. Imagine the faces of your proud mothers when they watch their talented offspring soar out over the audience. . .
92
The take-off is easy to master. Landings are a little harder–
CROCKETT JOHNSON
Cushlamochree!
SPLASH!
SPLASH!
SPLASH!
SPLASH!

And the parents will be here for the end-of-the-season festivities, Barnaby, and we can't have any more of the trouble this "Mr. O'Malley" of yours has been causing!
My Fairy Godfather didn't mean to—
9 3
The Smith boy—One of the children who fell in the lake with his clothes on—And we thought he'd caught a very slight cold—
Is he worse?
HE'S GOT CHICKEN POX!
Oh, NO!
Gosh!
CROCKETT JOHNSON
But I'm sure Mr. O'Malley didn't MEAN to give him chicken pox.

Mom and a lot of other parents are coming up to camp to see our show and Mrs. Krump's very upset because Joey Smith has chicken pox. He's in a separate bunkhouse so we won't get it. . .
04

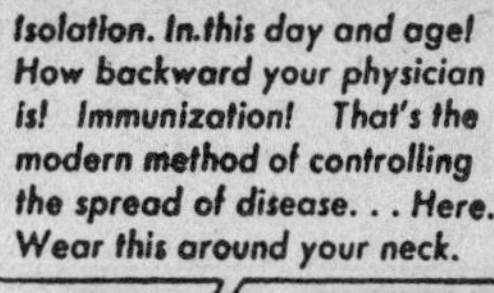
Isolation. In this day and age! How backward your physician is! Immunization! That's the modern method of controlling the spread of disease. . . Here. Wear this around your neck.

It's an ancient Druid magic charm for warding off the ravages of chicken pox. . .
It doesn't look old. . . . It looks kind of new. . .

It's very old, m'boy. It's been in my family alone over four years. I traded Third Cousin Malachy a used light bulb for it. . . . Told him it was a gazing crystal. . .
But now that you're immune, let us go and comfort Master Smith.
CROCKETT JOHNSON
Copyright 1943 Field Publications

Goodbye, Mrs. Krump. Barnaby had a grand summer at camp.
Goodbye.
The little entertainment the kids put on for us was wonderful. . .
'Bye.
Mr. O'Malley, my Fairy Godfather, never got here for the show. . . Something's happened!
KIDDIE KAM
Well. . . Everything went off smoothly enough. . . Even the kid's show . . . Poor Barnaby He expected that imaginary pixie to arrive in the midst of it and do card tricks! He actually expected him to. . .
Copyright 1943 Field Publications
CROCKETT JOHNSON
You know, Miss Pringle. . .
SO DID I!

Barnaby, what is that thing you have around your neck? Let me see it. . . "Souvenir of the New York World's Fair"
It's an old magic charm Mr. O'Malley, my Fairy Godfather, gave me. It stops you from getting chicken pox. That's why I didn't catch it from Joey Smith.
Mom! The next stop is right next to Mr. O'Malley's hotel. Let's get off and see why he wasn't at the camp show.
We're passing it now, Mom! Hear the jukebox? We'll get off at the station and get the next train—
Hush, Barnaby.
I see him! At the window! Mr. O'Malley!
CROCKETT JOHNSON
CHICKEN POX
MY WILD IRISH ROSE
CALLACHAN
Copyright 1943 Field Publications

I have to tell Gorgon about the Kiddie Kamp and Mr. O'Malley, my Fairy Godfather, and—
Okay, son.
9-8
Hey, Pop! It doesn't take long to get over chicken pox, does it? How long?
Oh, just a few—
Wait!
Barnaby imagines his "Fairy Godfather" has chicken pox! And he isn't likely to dream of visits from that pestiferous pixie if—
How long, Pop?
CROCKETT JOHNSON
Oh, just a few years.
Huh!
Copyright 1943 Field Publications

It doesn't take KIDS a couple of years to get over chicken pox, Pop. . . So why should—
It affects pixies differently, son. . . . But you've got to go to bed now.
9-9

But, gosh! I won't see Mr. O'Malley for years—
That's what we hope—I mean, we'll all hope for the best. . .

I feel so guilty. . . He believes everything we've told him . . .
That's the whole point! He believes his "Fairy Godfather" CAN'T come to see him so he won't imagine he DOES. It's logically impossible. . .

Copyright 1943 Field Publications
CROCKETT JOHNSON
Hello, m'boy.
Mr. O'Malley!

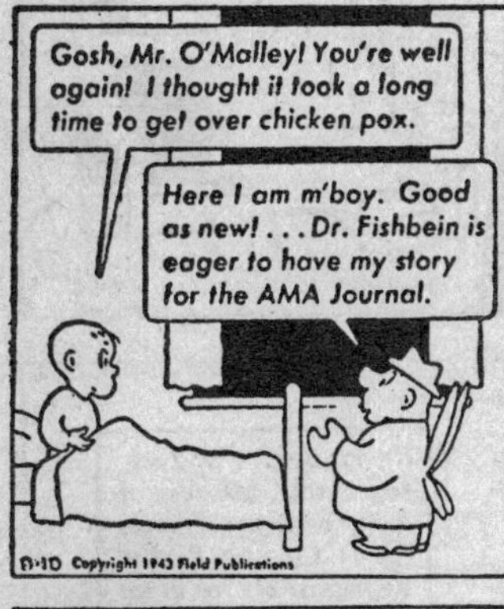
Gosh, Mr. O'Malley! You're well again! I thought it took a long time to get over chicken pox.
Here I am m'boy. Good as new! . . . Dr. Fishbein is eager to have my story for the AMA Journal.
Copyright 1943 Field Publications

As I lay there in the throes of the dread disease, my mind—still crystal clear—set itself to work devising a cure. Making use of all the newest medical findings, I jotted down a prescription and sent Gus out to get it filled. . .

It called for .0247 grains of sulfanilimide, half a gramme of sulfapyridine, a pinch of sulfathiazole, sulfaquanidine the size of a walnut, a jigger each of sulfasuxidine, sulfadiazine and sulfamolasses. . .
And it worked?

CROCKETT JOHNSON
No. But that hermit had a jug of Indian Herb Tonic... And well, m'boy here I am! Good as new!

A report on Barnaby's work at camp came today. Here it is.
I suppose it's pretty bad. Judging from what we've heard of the trouble he and his imaginary "Fairy Godfather" caused them.
8-11

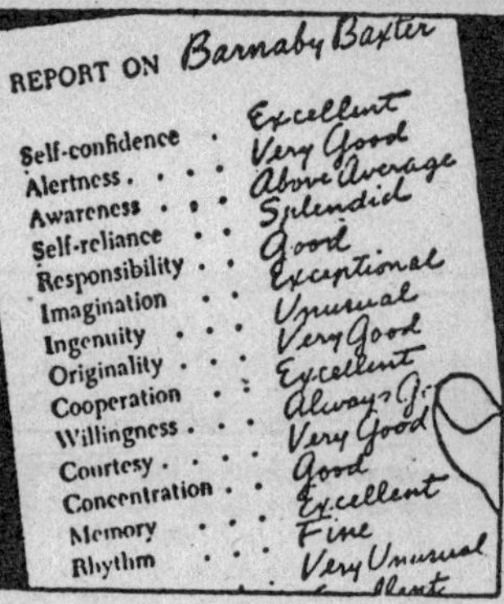
REPORT ON Barnaby Baxter
Self-confidence . Excellent
Alertness . . . . Very Good
Awareness . . . Above Average
Self-reliance . . Splendid
Responsibility . . Good
Imagination . . Exceptional
Ingenuity . . . Unusual
Originality . . . Very Good
Cooperation . . Excellent
Willingness . . . Always G
Courtesy . . . . Very Good
Concentration . . Good
Memory . . . Excellent
Rhythm . . . Fine
Very Unusual

Say! This is a fine report! Sounds as though he was Mrs. Krump's pet! We may have exaggerated all his "over-imaginativeness"—
Mrs. Krump sent a letter with it—

CROCKETT JOHNSON
Copyright 1943 Field Publications
It ends up. . . "and we regret that, because of many prior enrollments for next season, it will be impossible for us to have Barnaby with us."

I'm going downtown with Mom. She's going to the ration board for more sugar for canning and then we're going to the movies.
I must see the board, too. I lost my ration book. But now I'm due at the club.
D-13

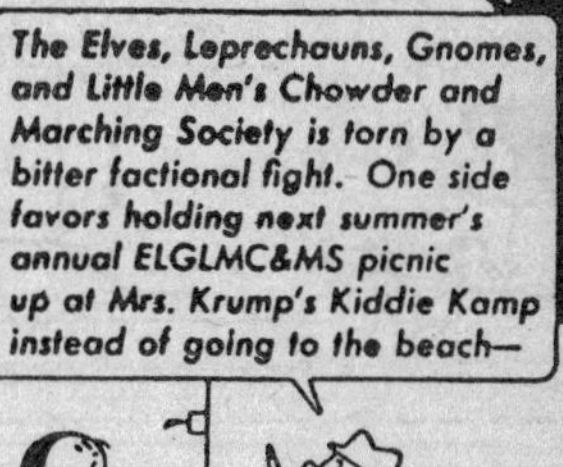
The Elves, Leprechauns, Gnomes, and Little Men's Chowder and Marching Society is torn by a bitter factional fight. One side favors holding next summer's annual ELGLMC&MS picnic up at Mrs. Krump's Kiddie Kamp instead of going to the beach—

Mr. O'Malley, I forgot to tell you. They don't want me at the Kiddie Kamp next year—
WHAT? . . . Well, Barnaby, that settles it! . . . I shall vote with the opposition!
Copyright 1943 Field Publications

That will make Jacob's Beach a unanimous choice . . . And I'll be able to get away in no time.
. . . See you at the ration board, m'boy.
CROCKETT JOHNSON

SUGAR APPLICATIONS
OPA
Hush, Barnaby.
But my Fairy Godfather IS coming here. . . . He lost his ration book. . .
Copyright 1943 Field Publications 9-14
CROCKETT JOHNSON
I'll wait out here for him.
Those 5000 ration books are in nice neat packages inside the office . . . This is a cinch!
Oh, here he comes!
Hello—Say! What's the driver of that car thinking of! . . . Leaving his engine racing like that in front of an OPA office! They'll take his A card away from him!

Leaving an engine running! And at this speed! . . . I'll adjust the carburetor before I shut it off . . .
Maybe the men won't want you fixing their car, Mr. O'Malley
9-15
They'll be awfully grateful—Say, this is an unusual carburetor . . . Quite different from the ones on Stanley Steamers . . . Fetch me a hammer, m'boy, or a large rock
The engine's stopped now.
I can't do a good job without the proper tools . . . I'll hail a passing motorist and try to borrow a turret lathe . . . Wait here, Barnaby. I'll be back . . .
CROCKETT JOHNSON
HOLD UP! POLICE!
Okay! Into the car and drive like—
Gosh!
Copyright 1943 Field Publications

The police caught them both!
There's a reporter!
RATION BOARD
It seems that a guy passing by yanked the distributor off the crooks' car.
9-16
You're all eye-witnesses? Anybody happen to know the modest gent who foiled the hold-up? His name?
J. J. O'Malley. He's my—
He was tall, with wavy brown hair.
"J. J. O'Malley"—Wait. One at a—
I hurried to assist him as he grappled with the thugs, but—
I saw him—
But—
CROCKETT JOHNSON
And THEN what did this O'Malley do?
ONE WAY
I saw him knock down one of the men and—
But, Mom! . . . I'm an eye-witness!
Copyright 1943 Field Publications

Why did that man who stopped the ration book robbery have to be named "O'Malley". . .Barnaby immediately got the notion it was HIS "Mr. O'Malley." He says he SAW that imaginary pixie wreck the hold-up men's car.
From the newspaper account, this J. J. O'Malley is more like The Lone Ranger . . ." Realizing a hold-up was in progress, he disabled the bandit car. When the heavily-armed thugs made their appearance, O'Malley, barehanded, accosted them both. . ."
9-17

"According to Miss Ada T. Giggins, an eye-witness, O'Malley stayed at the scene until he was sure the police had the situation in hand. Then, adjusting his cravat, and running his hand through his wavy brown hair, he quietly strolled off about his business."

What puzzles me, Barnaby, is Miss Ada T. Giggins and that wavy brown hair. I can't recall losing my hat in the struggle.
Copyright 1943 Field Publications
CROCKETT JOHNSON

Seen today's paper, Barnaby? Three items about your Fairy Godfather . . ." The attempted robbery, foiled by the quick and courageous action of a passerby, J. J. O'Malley of this city, has exposed a big black market ring here . . ."
9·18

Then an editorial entitled "We Need More O'Malleys" goes on to say, "Action—Not Talk is the motto of the modest private citizen who left the scene of his heroism to avoid the plaudits of the crowd Would that we had more people of his demeanor in public office."
Copyright 1943 Field Publications

Gosh. What's the third story, Mr. O'Malley?
This one doesn't mention me by name exactly. . .

CROCKETT JOHNSON
The headline reads, "SEEK CANDIDATE FOR CONGRESS" and I, well, m'boy—
Congress!

I see Boss Snagg hasn't chosen a candidate for our district's congressional vacancy yet . . .
Does Boss Snagg pick people to go to Congress, Pap?
The opposition candidate, Beauregard W. Mintleaf, got his campaign off to a flying start, lambasting Snagg's political machine.
Mintleaf has got a lot of money behind him. . . If Boss Snagg is going to win this year he's got to dig up somebody different from his usual political hacks.
Who can he run?
CROCKETT JOHNSON
Mr. O'Malley! Before you can go to Congress, you have to see Boss Snagg!
O'MALLEY FOR CONGRESS

Boss Snagg? . . . Not old Honest John Snagg? The eccentric philanthropist? . . . He'll be very eager to back me for Congress . . .
You know him, Mr. O'Malley?
D 21
I've been of assistance to him in his charity work. . . I discovered that once a year he practices an odd benevolence. . . He gives away two-dollar bills in a dark alley back of the political club. . .
And I've made a point of being on line each election day to add to the kindly gentleman's joy in giving. . . . So, you see, m'boy, he's quite indebted to me. . .
Copyright 1943 Field Publications
Also, a humanitarian of his type, always concerned with the common good, delights in seeing statesman of stature grasping—Hello?—the helm—
Hello! Honest John?
CROCKETT JOHNSON

It's a deal, then, Snagg. I'll duck out the back way. Can't be seen leaving the lair of my worst political enemy. . .

It's a deal, Mintleaf.

So we're blowing the special election for Congress, eh, Boss?
We couldn't win anyway, with that black market scandal breaking over us. . . But, from the size of Mintleaf's check, he doesn't know that. . .

We'll line up the boys as usual. But Election Day they'll vote for Mintleaf instead of for our guy. —Say! Who IS our candidate?
That's still a problem, Danny. . . . But there must be SOMEONE—
CROCKETT JOHNSON

There's a guy on the phone named O'Malley. . . Says he wants to run for Congress.

J. J. O'Malley...The honest citizen the papers gave the big hand last week when he mussed up that ration book heist... He says we should nominate him for Congress!
9 23

Yes, this is Honest John Snagg. Mmmm. . .I see. . .If we had an idea, Mr. O'Malley, of how far these backers of yours might go in—er—defraying the cost of your election campaign...
Boss. You can't

You see, Mr. O'Malley, I think a sizable contribution could easily sway the nomination in your favor. . . A check for—shall we say—$50,000 . . . ?
Whoops!
Copyright 1943 Field Publications

CROCKETT JOHNSON
Luckily, we won't need any cash at all, m'boy. Where does your dad keep his checkbook?
BANK

Call the papers and tell them our candidate for the special congressional election is none other than J. J. O'Malley, the people's choice! Look!
A check!
9-24
September 23 43
Bank and Trust Company
Honest John Snagg $50,000
Fifty thousand Dollars
J. J. O'Malley
We've already sold out the election to Mintleaf. And then this fall guy shows up, not only willing to run, but he kicks in with fifty grand!
I haven't met him yet, Danny, but I'll bet he has WINGS!
CROCKETT JOHNSON
Mr. O'Malley, don't people have to put money in the bank if they write checks?
Ssh, m'boy, I'm at work on a bill to revise the nation's financial methods.
Copyright 1943 Field Publications

We can set up headquarters for my whirlwind political campaign right here, m'boy.
But maybe Mom won't want anybody running for Congress from our cellar, Mr. O'Malley.
9-25

It will make your domicile immortal... Woodcuts of it in future history books. ...A plaque on the door... Posterity tramping in and out, swiping souvenirs...
But—

A fast telegram to Callaghan's Valhalla, Echo Lake: "NOW IS THE TIME FOR ALL GOOD MEN TO COME TO THE AID OF THEIR PARTY STOP J J O'MALLEY."
You're sending for Gus, the Ghost?

Yes. And I'm holding a confab of some of the wiser heads in the Elves, Leprechauns, Gnomes, and Little Men's Chowder and Marching Society here tonight. Ask your mother to leave out a platter of cold lamb canapés.
CROCKETT JOHNSON

John. That J. J. O'Malley who's running for Congress . . . Is his photograph in the newspapers?
No . . . Just a story about Boss Snagg nominating him.
I want his picture to show Barnaby that it's another Mr. O'Malley. And not his imaginary Fairy Godfather.
Say! That will convince him!
I must get these photos in the mail at once. To the papers and to Boss Snagg for the election posters. . . Fine artistic camera portraits, aren't they, m'boy?. . . Friend of mine took them. Very eminent passport photographer.

There's a photo of the O'Malley who's running for Congress in tonight's paper. . . We'll show it to Barnaby. . . When he's not able to recognize it, he'll agree it's not his "Fairy Godfather". . .
What does the real candidate look like?
9-28
Oh, he. looks like all the candidates Boss Snagg nominates—Say. . . What did I do with that paper?
Maybe you left it in the hall?
No, it's not here—
Hey, Mom! Pop! Look at this! . . .
CROCKETT JOHNSON
In the newspaper! . . . A picture of Mr. O'Malley, my Fairy Godfather!
Copyright 1943 Field Publications

But, Gus, look. Inflation is caused by people spending money, isn't it? So when my bill passes Congress, every man, woman and child are to get checkbooks. . . They'll put all their money in War Bonds and spend checks! . . .
Your plan might get you votes. But as John Maynard Keynes points out—Hello, little boy. . .
Mr. O'Malley—Oh, hello, Gus.
9-29
Copyright 1943 Field Publications
Pop says people get put in jail when they write checks if they haven't got money in the bank.
A discriminatory law! Penalizing only the poor! When I'm elected I'll—er—What? JAIL?
CROCKETT JOHNSON
O'Malley! YOU haven't been writing checks?. . .
Yes, he has. That's why I asked Pop.

Boss, when Mintleaf paid you to throw the special congressional election you told him you'd run a "political nonentity" against him. . . You sure kept your word.
One of the reasons they refer to me as Honest John Snagg.
9-30

But we've got to make this guy O'Malley look like a reasonable facsimile of a candidate. . . The papers keep calling us for dope on him and we've never even seen him! We haven't got his address! His name's not in the phone book or city directory—

His name IS on his $50,000 check for "campaign expenses."
Say! I can reach him through the bank. . .

CROCKETT JOHNSON
Boss. . . The bank says O'Malley has no account there!
Copyright 1943 Field Publications

Call up Boss Snagg, Gus. Explain that the check I sent him was—er—only a symbolic gesture of my good will, and not to be deemed a thing of—er—intrinsic or real value. . . . He'll understand. . .
10-1

A phony check! There MUST be a mistake. Nobody would do such a thing to me, would they, Danny? Not to old Honest John Snagg!
Not if they wanted to live—That's your phone ringing, Boss.
Copyright 1943 Field Publications

He'll tell me not to give the $50,000 a second thought. . .
This is J. J. O'Malley's secretary, Mr. Snagg. I want to explain—Oh!

CROCKETT JOHNSON
Don't even think once about it, O'Malley! Hurry! Get him that $50,000 right away! In cash!
. . . or else!

So, there's nothing to do but borrow the $50,000. . . I hate to impose on your parents, but—
I did ask Pop, but he said he was a little bit short this week—
10-8

Barnaby! You asked him to come to my financial aid! What must he think of me! "A FINE Fairy Godfather, my son has got," he'll tell the boys at the office. "Tried to nick me for fifty grand! Put the kid up to asking me!"

Weren't you going to ask me to ask him, Mr. O'Malley?. . .
Perish the thought, Barnaby. . .
Copyright 1943 Field Publications

I'm negotiating this loan at the Convivial Credit Company. I was merely going to ask you to ask him to be a co-signer.
CROCKETT JOHNSON

Won't you get in more trouble if you borrow the money to give Boss Snagg, Mr. O'Malley? You'll have to pay the loan man back—
By that time I'll be elected, m'boy.
Zzzzzzz.
10-4

And I can claim congressional immunity . . . How else can I get the money? I'm not likely to be stumbling over $50,000 as I stroll along—Cushlamochree!
Look out!

Copyright 1943 Field Publications
Hey! Me treasure chest! . . . O'Malley! Don't you never look where you're going?
The invisible leprechaun!
McSnoyd!

That McSnoyd! Leaving his treasure chest out where it's a menace to life and limb—
Er—Barnaby! A treasure! My good old pal, McSnoyd!
CROCKETT JOHNSON

McSnoyd, I suppose you know I've been prevailed upon to run in the special election for Congress in the district.
I hoid about it, O'Malley. It give me a laugh in the midst of all me troubles . . .
10-5
I won't bother you with any of the complex details, McSnoyd, old pal, but I now find myself obligated to Boss Snagg for a substantial sum of money and—
What boins me up is I can't get to the Woild's Series . . .
Watching over this here box of money twenty-four hours a day . . . Can't procure the soivices of nobody for this non-essential occupation. . .·. Oh, the boiden of riches!
Er—McSnoyd . . .
Copyright 1943 Field Publications
We always have trouble with that invisible leprechaun . . .
Hush, m'boy . . . McSnoyd, I'll be glad to—er—take care of your treasure. . . You go to the ball game.
My pal!

M'boy, your old Fairy Godfather put one over on McSnoyd this time. There he goes, off to the ball game, and we've got his treasure . . . Let's examine it . . .
I bet there's a catch to this . . .
10-6
Copyright 1943 Field Publications
A trunk full of two-dollar bills! . . . I'll take $50,000 of it for Boss Snagg and the O'Malley-for-Congress campaign—$2—$4—$6—
But, gosh . . .
$49,996—$49,998—$50,000— —$50,002! I'll take this last bill, too, for any incidentals that may crop up . . . And the trunk to carry the $50,000 . . .
Isn't this "stealing," Mr. O'Malley? . . .
It's all legal and above board, m'boy, to outwit a leprechaun. . . . We'll have the expressman get the trunk at your house and deliver it to Boss Snagg.
I bet there IS a catch to this . . .
CROCKETT JOHNSON

Boss. The expressman left a trunk . . . $1.22, collect. I paid for it . . . But it's full of two-dollar bills! And—
O'Malley finally has kicked in with his "campaign" money!
10-7

You're our candidate for city treasurer, aren't you, Muggins? Can you count?
Sure, Boss. —One—Two—Three—Four—

Fine. Count those bills and see if there's $50,000 . . . Then put a thousand in the black bag in the safe to pay the boys on election day and lock the rest up in my safe deposit vault . . .
Okay, Boss. But . . .
Copyright 1943 Field Publications

But what, Muggins?
I was just going to say, ain't two-dollar bills kind of unlucky?
CROCKETT JOHNSON

Now that Boss Snagg and I are again on amicable terms he'll loose an avalanche of O'Malley-for-Congress ads, handbills, posters, banners—
Here's Jane . . .
Barnaby. They put a picture of your Fairy Godfather up on Hanson's old cowbarn . . .
No doubt Mintleaf's puny poster pales beside my display . . .
Wait until I polish up my glasses, O'Malley
O'MALLEY FOR CONGRESS
MINTLEAF
FOR CONGRESS
CROCKETT JOHNSON
Copyright 1943 Field Publications

MINTLEAF
MINTLEAF
MINTLEAF
MINTLEAF
FOR CONGRESS
MINTLEAF
10-8

MINTLEAF
FOR
CONGRESS
MINTLEAF

Mintleaf
Copyright 1943 Field Publications

MINTLEAF
Mom! Look!
O'MALLEY FOR CONGRESS

—and your commentator has a thought on one aspect of the special congressional contest: The strikingly frugal campaign budget of J. J. O'Malley and—
Perhaps if I add this $2 to the fund—
10-11
—the lavish expenditures of his opponent, Beauregard Mintleaf. I believe many thinking voters, when they reflect that this is a time for stringent economy,—
You know, that occurred to me—
Copyright 1943 Field Publications
—will agree with this observer that O'Malley's modest campaign is as shrewd as it is patriotic . . . Economy is the watchword today. So get Conkle's Confetti in the large, two-dollar, economy size—
Mmmm . . . I'll have to run downtown, m'boy.
What for, Mr. O'Malley?
For a large box of Conkle's Confetti . . . I'll need it for my victory celebration.
CROCKETT JOHNSON

Barnaby. I bear sad tidings.
Couldn't you get any confetti for the party you're going to have when you're elected?
10-12
Copyright 1943 Field Publications

I didn't go directly to the confetti emporium . . . I had an idea, enroute, whereby it seemed that two-dollar bill might be transformed into a six-dollar bill. So I hastened to the track . . .
And you lost . . .

The man at the $2 window refused my wager! Claimed my banknote was spurious! . . . Bogus! . . . COUNTERFEIT!
Gosh!

Then maybe all the money you got from the leprechaun and sent to Boss Snagg to elect you to Congress is no good!
CUSHLAMOCHREE!
CROCKETT JOHNSON

That leprechaun! Allowing me to take his treasure to defray the expenses of my campaign for Congress! Knowing it was worthless! . . . Jeopardizing my promising political career! . . .
Gosh, Mr. O'Malley.
10-13
But maybe the man was wrong about the money being no good.
I doubt it, m'boy. . . . But we might check . . . Has your encyclopedia got pictures in it?
The controversy hinged on the authenticity of the portrait engraved on the face of the note. He seemed so certain of his facts that I didn't continue the argument after he beckoned to the uniformed patrolman . . .
Barnaby! He was wrong! This money is all right!
. . . Jefferson Davis did NOT have a mustache!
CROCKETT JOHNSON

I had Gus fix up a few slightly used placards we found in the cellar of Callaghan's Valhalla. Like to see them, m'boy?
Sure, Mr. O'Malley.
10-14

CROCKETT JOHNSON
Tippecanoe & O'MALLEY Too
O'MALLEY IS JUST AROUND THE CORNER
MUGWUMP O'MALLEY

Just the thing for the terrific spontaneous demonstration I expect will follow my address at the Elves, Leprechauns, Gnomes and Little Men's Chowder and Marching Society tonight . . .
Gosh!
TAXATION WITHOUT O'MALLEY IS TYRANNY
KNOW NOTHING O'MALLEY
GRASS ROOTS O'MALLEY
SINGLE TAX O'MALLEY
BULLMOOSE O'MALLEY
54-40 OR O'MALLEY

Snagg! I paid you to lose this election! Are you crossing me up with this man O'Malley?
Mintleaf, we haven't lifted a finger for J. J. O'Malley.
10-15

Yes! . . . Listen! "Seldom has a congressional race captured voters' imaginations as has O'Malley's 'Silent Campaign' and Mintleaf's frantic and costly effort to combat it . . ."

". . . O'Malley's reticence, which has won him the intriguing and vote-getting titles of 'Nebulous Nominee' and 'Mystery Candidate' is a master stroke of the old political wizard, Boss Snagg . . ."
But you wanted him kept quiet.
Copyright 1943 Field Publications

Please, Snagg . . . Make him talk!
If you'd care—er—to write a check for his radio time, I might be able to coax him to speak on the air.
CROCKETT JOHNSON

O'Malley! You're going on the air! . . . "Mystery Candidate to Break Silence . . . O'Malley on radio next Saturday in his first public speech of campaign."
Gosh!
My FIRST speech? . . . The sublime ignorance of these newspapers! I've made six public speeches at the Elves, Leprechauns, Gnomes, and Little Men's Chowder and Marching Society so far! Why don't they send reporters there?
10-18
It's been years since a journalist has visited that fountainhead of vital news—except that reporter-at-large from The New Yorker . . . When did you say I'm to give this little radio chat, Gus?—Saturday?
CROCKETT JOHNSON
Can't make it! . . . I have another very momentous oration to deliver at the ELG&LMC&M Society . . .
But, O'Malley!

I've solved the problem of those conflicting speaking dates, m'boy. I'll TRANSCRIBE my radio talk. . . It can be broadcast Saturday and I'll make my important oration to the Elves, Leprechauns, Gnomes, and Little Men at the Chowder and Marching Society in person.
Hello, Mr. O'Malley.
Barnaby. Why does your Fairy Godfather make speeches to those Little Men? . . . They can't vote.
10-18
Copyright 1943 Field Publications
They can't vote? How little the child knows of politics! . . . I must rush off to make that record or I'd explain—
Where are you going to make it, Mr. O'Malley?
Menlo Park. . . I hear that fellow Edison who invented the jukebox also perfected an astounding device for recording the human voice.

I made a record once, Barnaby. When I was three years old. I used to get a nickel if I sang Ding Dong Bell for company.. Then my father got this thing for our radio and he gave me a dime for singing into it...
10-19
Copyright 1943 Field Publications.
After that they just played the record for the company.
Didn't Mr. Petrillo do anything—But, say! Is this apparatus still in your home, little girl?
Pop uses it to make records of what the commentators on the radio say is going to happen. Then he plays them over six months afterward.
How fiendish! But, come...
This is indeed fortuitous!... I can transcribe my speech right here in Jane's house.
Is Gorgon invited in too, Jane?
But—
CROCKETT JOHNSON

A pity your folks are not home to hear me transcribing this epoch-making radio speech. . .
I'll put a record on, Barnaby. Your Fairy Godfather just has to talk into that. . .
10-20

As I stand here before you, my unseen multitude of friends, I find myself echoing phrases of another immortal statesman—
Tsk! Forgot my notes!

CROCKETT JOHNSON
Is there a copy of the collected speeches of Edmund Burke in the bookcase, little girl?
Mr. O'Malley. The record is still going. . .
Huh?

Perhaps I had better tell a humorous joke at this juncture. . . Haven't you a set of bound volumes of Captain Billy's Whizbang?
Ahem. . .

"... The one absolutely unselfish friend that a man can have in this selfish world, the one that never deserts him, the one that never proves ungrateful ... is his dog! Gentlemen of the Jury: A man's dog stands by him in prosperity and in poverty, in health and—
10-21

Hush, m'boy. I must find an apt quotation before I can go on. Something in Latin...
But the record machine is going and nobody is saying anything into it.
BEN HUR

Copyright 1943 Field Publications
"the noble dog ... his head between his paws, his eyes sad but open in alert watchfulness, faithful and true...

CROCKETT JOHNSON
Mr. O'Malley, I think the record's run out.
Nonsense. I'm just beginning my oration...

and in closing, I want my unseen audience to rise and sing three stanzas of my campaign hymn, "O Tempora, O Mores, O'Malley"—
Mr. O'Malley. This record was filled a long time ago.
10-22

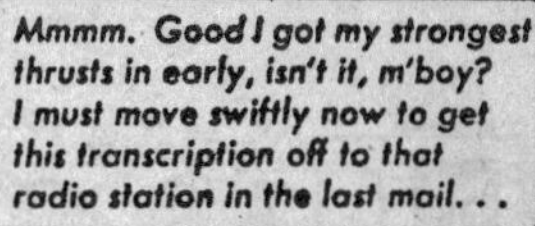
Mmmm. Good I got my strongest thrusts in early, isn't it, m'boy? I must move swiftly now to get this transcription off to that radio station in the last mail. . .

Aren't you going to play it over?

What could be wrong with it? Anyway, I can always claim I was misquoted. . . Where are the stamps, little girl? . . . Ah! I've found a book of them. . . Thirty brown points will do it.

CROCKETT JOHNSON
Copyright 1943 Field Publications
Well, Barnaby. That's that!
US MAIL

Mintleaf finally has smoked out his silent opponent. O'Malley has to take a stand on SOMETHING in his first broadcast tonight. . .
Isn't it time for his speech?
10-23

I find myself echoing phrases of another immortal statesman—
He's playing safe. Taking his line on important issues from some bigshot.

—Ahem. Gentlemen of the Jury: The best friend a man has—
Hasn't his voice changed?
Gentlemen of the Jury?

Copyright 1943 Field Publications
CROCKETT JOHNSON
. . . the noble dog . . . faithful and true—
Say! He's quoting Senator G. G. Vest's Eulogy of the Dog! The whole thing!

Half the people in town think O'Malley, by not deigning to answer Mintleaf's campaign arguments and spending his radio time reciting Senator Vest's "Eulogy of the Dog," did a clever job of disparagement
10-28
Copyright 1943 Field Publications
CROCKETT JOHNSON
I think it was a very cynical stunt, John.
And the other half took him straight . . . They're dog lovers.
I don't believe it. I'm sure Mr. Mintleaf isn't worried in the least by O'Malley's undignified tricks. And—
Mintleaf's press agent is. Look.
MINTLEAF LOVES DOGS, TOO
SPCA

Copyright 1943 Field Publications
CROCKETT JOHNSON
So my esteemed opponent says I don't dare face issues? . . . Well, Gus, what will he say to my bold challenge to him to debate these issues publicly? . . . At the Elves, Leprechauns, Gnomes and Little Men's Chowder and Marching Society . . .
I'll run over now and arrange things . . .
But, O'Malley. You can't do ALL your campaigning there.
10-26

. . . special congressional election in this district . . . J. J. O'Malley, making his first appearance of his amazing campaign, will face Candidate Mintleaf on the stage.
He arranged it already!

The debate is expected to draw a record crowd to Town Hall . . .
Town Hall!

But, Pop, Mr. O'Malley, my Fairy Godfather, said he was going to debate his esteemed opponent at the Little Men's Club . . . And—
Barnaby. The two candidates for Congress are having their debate at Town Hall! . . . And that imaginary pixie of yours is NOT one of the candidates!
10-27
There's one way to convince him, Ellen. Attend the debate!
Swell, Pop! But first I'll have to see Mr. O'Malley.
Copyright 1943 Field Publications
CROCKETT JOHNSON
. . . And ask him how to get to the Little Men's Club.

MINTLEAF
for
CONGRESS
There's Mintleaf . . .
Where's O'Malley?
Pop—

CROCKETT
JOHNSON
MINTLEAF
for
CONG
He's still backstage,
I imagine . . . Planning
a dramatic entrance.
I'll see
if he is.

A door with a star on
it. My Fairy Godfather
is probably in here . . .
DRESSING ROOM
Copyright 1943 Field Publications

EEEK! . . . Goodness! You
startled me, little boy . . .
Oh, dear! Is it time now?
Already? For me to make
O'Malley's speech for him?
Gus!
O'MALLEY
FOR
CONGRESS

Your Fairy Godfather felt that half the debate should be held at the Little Men's Chowder and Marching Society. He's there . . .
And you're going to debate for him here?
O'MALLEY FOR CONGRESS
10-29
Yes. But—oh, dear—why did I permit O'Malley to talk me into it? That big audience—And I had such an upsetting adventure as I passed the cemetery on my way here . . .
Copyright 1943 Field Publications
Two ghoulish figures! Huddled up against the headstones and writing in big books the shape of voters' registers . . . Hideous creatures! Like Boss Snagg's ruffians! What an experience!
I can't face that audience out there tonight, little boy. I'm a bundle of nerves. I can't do it!
But, Gus, gosh! Somebody has to make a speech to get Mr. O'Malley elected!
CROCKETT JOHNSON

. . . my opponent, J. J. O'Malley, has not dared come here tonight to refute my arguments because he CANNOT refute them! Nor can ANYONE refute them—
MINTLEAF for CONGRESS
Pardon. Is this seat taken? . . .
Huh?

I'm going to debate because Mr. O'Malley couldn't come and—
Turn out the lights!
Barnaby!

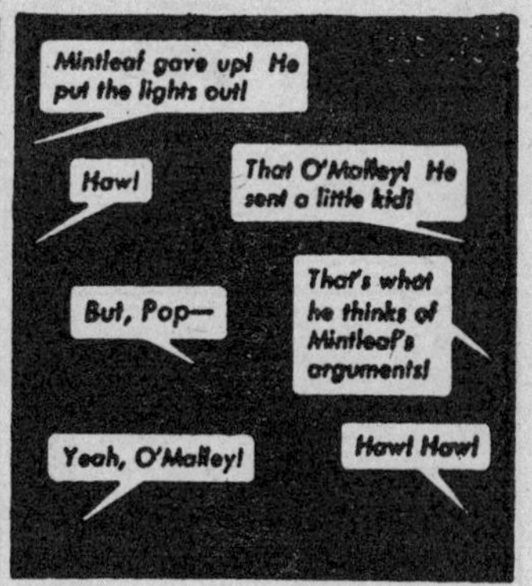
Mintleaf gave up! He put the lights out!
Haw!
That O'Malley! He sent a little kid!
But, Pop—
That's what he thinks of Mintleaf's arguments!
Yeah, O'Malley!
Haw! Haw!

Boss! That O'Malley—that fall guy candidate of yours—he's made Mintleaf look like a sap so often they're quoting him at even money. If we switch our floaters to him, he'll win—
And double-cross Mintleaf? After he's paid me to lose the election? . . . Danny! Do you think I—Honest John Snagg—would do anything like that? With the dough I've got bet on Mintleaf? . . .
Copyright 1942, Field Publications
Have the boys in the alley ready to start voting early and often for Mintleaf. I'll be there to pay them off. . . with some of the two-dollar bills O'Malley provided. . .
Okay, Boss. But—
CROCKETT JOHNSON
Very reassuring item in the paper, m'boy. . . "Boss John Snagg confident of outcome of election". . .

These deuces Boss Snagg give us to vote for Mintleaf! Look!
Confederate money! Hey!
They're phonies!
The BUM!
A outrage! Leave us heave some rocks through Snagg's window!
First, leave us get even by voting for O'MALLEY!
Yeh! . . . VOTE FOR O'MALLEY!
POLIT
CLU
11-2

CROCKETT JOHNSON
Mintleaf? I just paid off the boys. You're as good as in . . . O'Malley hasn't got a trick left in his hand. . .
O'MALLEY FOR CONGRESS
Copyright 1943 Field Publications
What? Wave my magic wand and assure my election? It wouldn't be fair, m'boy—Say! I'd better stroll by the polls and see if those Gnomes are still pulling the right lever. . . .
Okay, Mr. O'Malley.

Barnaby! Have you seen the papers? The election returns? . . .
Cushlamochree!
Huh? What? Oh, good morning, Mr. O'Malley.
11-3
Copyright 1943 Field Publications
What a blow to my prestige! I'll demand a recount! . . .
Didn't you get elected? Gosh!
Of COURSE I was elected. . .
O'MALLEY ELECTED!
CROCKETT JOHNSON
But I'd hoped it would be fairly close to UNANIMOUS! . . . And these tallies barely indicate a LANDSLIDE. . .

O'Malley elected! It's not possible! It couldn't have happened! How—
Boss! . . . A couple of torpedoes are here for the dough you bet on Mintleaf! That fifty grand is all Confederate money! Our boys are burned because you paid them off with it! We've elected a mug we've never seen—
O'MALLEY FOR CONGRESS
11-4
Copyright 1943 Field Publications
—Mintleaf swears you double-crossed him and I heard he's hired an out-of-town mob to—
BOSS!
I suppose this is as befitting a time as any, m'boy, to drop in on Boss Snagg and exchange felicitations on my victory. . .
I guess so, Mr. O'Malley.
CROCKETT JOHNSON

Let me rest here alone, Danny. Leave the window open . . . Air. To clear my head while I think our way out of this mess. . . The old brain will see something—
11-5
I'll make a simple speech. "Thank you, Honest John," I'll say, "for your help in electing me to Congress." Then I'll clasp his hand. . .
EEEOOWWW! Help! I saw a—
Cushlamochree! Where did Honest John go?. . .
Four blocks up that way, Mr. O'Malley. . . And around a corner.
CROCKETT JOHNSON

Yes. Boss Snagg's behavior yesterday was a bit odd. . . jumping out a window as I greeted him. . . I daresay the great responsibility of getting me elected to Congress was a strain. . .
11-6

Look, Ellen. . . If his machine had LOST the election I'd be able to understand this. . .

FINAL
SNAGG RETIRES FROM POLITICS
Political Boss Leaves Town
FOR HEALTH, FRIENDS SAY

CROCKETT JOHNSON
Take my word for it. . . There's an extraordinary story behind all that. . .

Barnaby, do you still insist our new Congressman is that pink-winged little pixie you imagine you see around here?
Mr. O'Malley? Sure, Mom . . .
11-8

Mr. O'Malley and his secretary, Gus the Ghost, are here right now. In our cellar. Having tea.
Oh, Barnaby!

A Congressman couldn't be in our cellar. Congress is in session and he'd be THERE, making laws and—
He should be in Congress? Gosh!
CROCKETT JOHNSON

After that strenuous campaign, it's nice to be able to relax, isn't it, Gus? Until next election—
Mr. O'Malley!

Mr. O'Malley! You got elected to Congress and Mom says you should BE there, making laws—
Of course! Congress!

I'd forgotten about that part of my job—Gus! As my secretary, you must remind me of these details—
Oh, dear—

Mr. O'Malley is leaving right away, Mom. He—
He's really leaving? Then you won't see that pixie anymore? You won't imagine—
CROCKETT JOHNSON

Copyright 1943 Field Publications
How can I see Mr. O'Malley when he's in Congress? . . . That's impossible, isn't it?
But Congressmen get Saturday and Sunday off, don't they, Mom?

Well, Barnaby . . . Time for your Fairy Godfather to depart for Congress . . . Gus has gone on ahead. Hitch-hiking . . . But I'm—
Haven't you gone yet, Mr. O'Malley? You should have—

Copyright 1943 Field Publications
I daresay my colleagues ARE messing things up without me. And I should be there helping them . . . But I wanted to make sure you realize the Nation's gain is not your loss, m'boy . . .

My seat in Congress is an ideal vantage point for watching over your interests . . . And, of course, you'll feel quite free to call on me for anything—a Post Office, or a dam, or copies of my speeches—
Can he get us a pony?

I'll draw up a bill right now . . . "HR procurement act to provide Jane and Barnaby with a pony—"
But, Mr. O'Malley! You've got to hurry to Congress! Gosh!
CROCKETT JOHNSON

It took a special election, but we're rid of that imaginary Fairy Godfather . . . He's gone to Congress, Barnaby says . . .
Fine. But we'll keep our fingers crossed.

Mr. O'Malley! I told Mom you left for Congress . . .
Barnaby! Get that large eraser from your drawing set!

. . . Luckily I happened to notice this just as I was departing . . . Look! . . . Vandalism! Mustaches! Undoubtedly the work of that Leprechaun, Launcelot McSnoyd!
But the election is over . . .
O'MALLEY for CONGRESS
CROCKETT JOHNSON

. . . And you should be in Congress.
Yes! Where I'm needed so direly! That McSnoyd! Holding me up like this!
O'MALLEY for CONGRESS
O'MALLEY for CONGRESS
Copyright 1943 Field Publications

I hate to cut short the historic occasion of my departure for Congress—Cushlamochree!
There's my plane!
Gosh!
Airline people said I couldn't be accomodated . . . All space taken . . . I told them there'd have to be a second section . . .
I'm the second section . . . Goodbye, Barnaby Goodbye, little girl . . .
Goodbye, Mr. O'Malley!
Goodbye.
Gosh! He really left this time . . .
CROCKETT JOHNSON

11-13
My Fairy Godfather probably has passed a lot of big laws by now, Pop. Hasn't the radio said anything about it yet?
A TRIPLE WINGBACK "T" FORMATION TO THE LEFT FROM A BALANCED LINE TO THE RIGHT WITH DEUCES WILD — IT WILL BE A KICK — OR A PASS — OR A RUNNING PLAY —

Not the comics, Mom. Read the front page. Isn't there anything about Mr. O'Malley in Congress.
No, Barnaby.

Don't you think it's funny we haven't heard anything about Mr. O'Malley since he left, Jane?
No—Look, Barnaby. . . . Here comes that dopey Ghost. He's back from Congress.
CROCKETT JOHNSON

Little boy! Where is your Fairy Godfather? He never arrived in Washington! . . .
Gosh!
Copyright 1943 Field Publications

Something must have happened to Mr. O'Malley, Gus. When Mom gets home she'll call the cops—
Oh! You suspect foul play! Perhaps we shouldn't wait.
11 15

Hello? Missing Persons Bureau? I'm reporting the disappearance of Congressman J. J. O'Malley . . . Blue eyes . . . A ruddy complexion . . . Two feet eleven inches tall—
And wings.

No, officer, TWO eleven . . . And pink wings—What? I beg your pardon, officer, I didn't catch—
CLICK
Somebody's in the kitchen! The icebox—

CROCKETT JOHNSON
Mr. O'Malley!
Copyright 1943 Field Publications

I'm glad you're all right Mr. O'Malley. But Mom says when Congressmen don't go to Congress it's a form of Absenteeism—
And it's shockingly prevalent! In fact, none of my fellow members showed up at ALL! Not ONE of them! . . . I've been introducing bills, arguing them pro and con, and passing them—by a narrow margin—for three lonely days!
But, O'Malley' There must be some mistake—
11 16 Copyright 1943 Field Publications
It was no mistake when THIS district elected the one conscientious, alert, and able statesman in Congress . . . By the way, m'boy, here's a postcard of the nation's Capitol.
Gosh.
CROCKETT JOHNSON
My goodness, O'Malley! Is this where you were? . . . It's Independence Hall! In Philadelphia!

These governmental shifts! . . .
How can ANYONE keep up
with them? And now you say
they've moved Congress from
Philadelphia to Washington!
Yes. In 1800 . . . And, O'Malley, there's
no place for us to live in Washington.
The city is dreadfully overcrowded . . .
CROCKETT
JOHNSON
11 17
If the government found
room there, Gus, surely
we can. Our requirements
are much more modest . . .
All we need is a small
twenty-room cote close
to the center of things. . .
Just leave it to me . . .
But, O'Malley—
Maybe he'll wave
his magic wand . . .

You've been exaggerating the housing shortage in the Capital, Gus . . . Lots of places to rent in this Washington paper I picked up in the Elves, Leprechauns, Gnomes, and Little Men's Chowder and Marching Society reading room . . . Here's one at Massachusetts and Connecticut Avenues . . .
A vacant apartment? Dear me! Amazing!
11 18
Copyright 1943 Field Publications

It's a house . . . With grounds. "18 rooms, 6 baths, ballroom, conservatory, lawns with iron deer, servants' quarters, large stables" . . . Sounds all right. Of course, it has no hunting preserve . . . Just iron deer . . .
CROCKETT JOHNSON
But I think you might go and look the place over, Gus, and— Say! Look at this headline . . . Great news from the Pacific!
". . . ADMIRAL DEWEY CAPTURES MANILA!"

Our new Congressman was elected to the Committee on Disposition of Useless Executive Papers . . . I suppose it's a very necessary job but it does sound a bit funny . . .
Gosh!
11 19

Mr. O'Malley! Pop read in the paper that you got elected to a committee in Congress . . .
Already? I didn't expect them to begin forcing the chairmanship of all the important committees upon me until I arrived in Washington. . . . What committee is it? Foreign Affairs? Rules? Appropriations?
Copyright 1943 Field Publications

CROCKETT JOHNSON
You're on the USELESS PAPERS COMMITTEE!

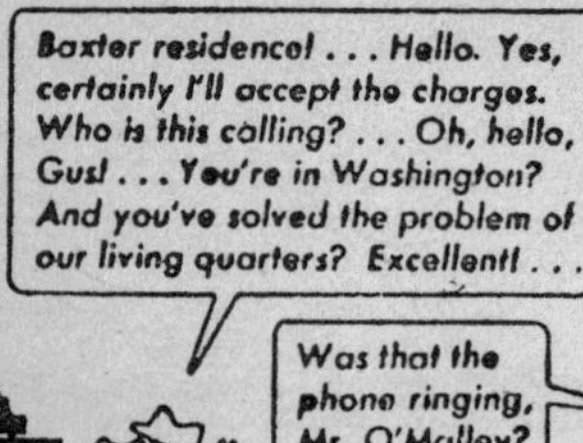
Baxter residence! . . . Hello. Yes, certainly I'll accept the charges. Who is this calling? . . . Oh, hello, Gus! . . . You're in Washington? And you've solved the problem of our living quarters? Excellent! . . .
Was that the phone ringing, Mr. O'Malley?

Oh, you've heard of my election to the Useless Papers Committee in Congress . . . Thank you, Gus. Yes, I intend to start working on it very soon . . . But what about the domicile you've procured for us? I hope it's not TOO ostentatious—

We'll plan a housewarming. Just a small party. Only ambassadors and cabinet members . . . What? Yes! I SAID I'd get to work on those Useless Papers! I realize it's important, but . . . What's that? If I clear out enough of them—

—we can live in a storeroom in the subcellar of the Capitol?
GUS!
Gosh! Are you going to live in the Capitol, Mr. O'Malley?

CROCKETT JOHNSON
Here's a report on the way the local Congressmen voted on important issues this month. Let's see what O'Malley did... "Absent," "Absent," "Absent!" He hasn't been there at ALL!
I'm going to write him a letter! I'll explain to him his job is to represent us—
Mr. O'Malley? My Fairy Godfather? I'll tell him, Pop...
11-28
He had some trouble finding a place to live in Washington. But he's going there soon...
Quiet, Barnaby.
I'm addressing this to him in Washington and sarcastically marking it, "Please forward." He'll get it—where's a stamp?
You won't need a stamp, Pop... If I hand it to him.

Ellen! . . . That letter I sent to our absent Congressman! Look!
It came back? . . . Why didn't they forward it to where he lives?
11 23

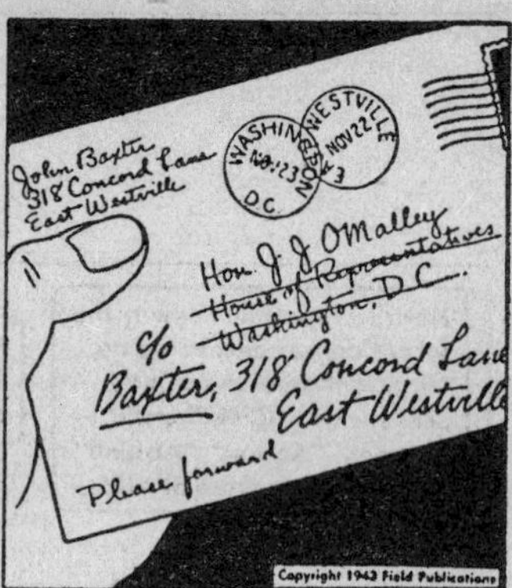
John Baxter
318 Concord Lane
East Westville
Hon. J. J. O'Malley
House of Representatives
Washington, D.C.
c/o Baxter, 318 Concord Lan
East Westvill
Please forward
Copyright 1943 Field Publications

Some absent-minded clerk put my return address on it instead of his and sent it to him here! Of all the impossible — Oh, I give up!
Pop!

Mr. O'Malley, my Fairy Godfather, just left for Congress. He says if any mail comes for him here to please forward it . . .
CROCKETT JOHNSON

Gosh, Mr. O'Malley! . . . You're back from Congress already!
Thanksgiving recess. I'm resting up before I start investigating a national scandal!
11-24
Copyright 1943 Field Publications
While performing the duties of the Committee on Disposition of Executive Papers, I came upon a document which apparently had been approved by Congress some time back . . . I was astounded! . . .
When Gus returned from the Potomac where he'd gotten rid of a pile of old letters from a fellow named Button Gwinnett, I showed it to him. Gus stood aghast! It was for a postoffice in Indiana for SANTA CLAUS!
Can you imagine, m'boy! A postoffice for a myth! A legendary character!
Are you going to investigate SANTA CLAUS?
CROCKETT JOHNSON

But, Mr. O'Malley, maybe Santa Claus needs that postoffice Congress gave him . . . Gosh, with all the letters kids write him just before Christmas . . .
Barnaby! You amaze me! Surely you know Santa Claus is merely a myth! A folk legend! A hoax perpetrated on kiddies!
11-25
Copyright 1943 Field Publications

If Santa Claus was real—if anyone had ever seen him—
I've seen him Mr. O'Malley.
Barnaby. Has anyone ever spoken to you about that imagination of yours? . . .
But—
CROCKETT JOHNSON

Maybe Santa Claus HAS got a postoffice, Barnaby. Up at the North Pole—
No. In Indiana.
11 27
There's the TOWN of Santa Claus in Indiana, son. And I imagine it has a postoffice. But where did you hear—
He has a whole town?
Copyright 1943 Field Publications
CROCKETT JOHNSON
Mr. O'Malley! I have some news for your committee investigating Santa Claus!
Not now .... Gus and I are off on a momentous matter involving a couple of vital branches of the government.
MAMMOTH CAVE
NAVY
ARMY

Jane, you've seen Santa Claus, too, haven't you? . . . Mr. O'Malley doesn't believe I saw him—
Sure. I've seen him.
Cushlamochree! It's impossible! . . . You've both seen him! . . . This calls for a REAL investigation! I'd expected to be able to confine the work of the "Congressional Committee to Investigate Santa Claus" to encyclopedia research.
11-26
Copyright 1943 Field Publications
But now the committee must ask Congress for funds to widen its scope . . . I'm sure the revelation of the— er— "O'Malley Committee," as it will be called on the front pages, will rock the nation!
CROCKETT JOHNSON
And how would you like to aid in this important patriotic service . . . As special investigators?
Huh?
Huh?

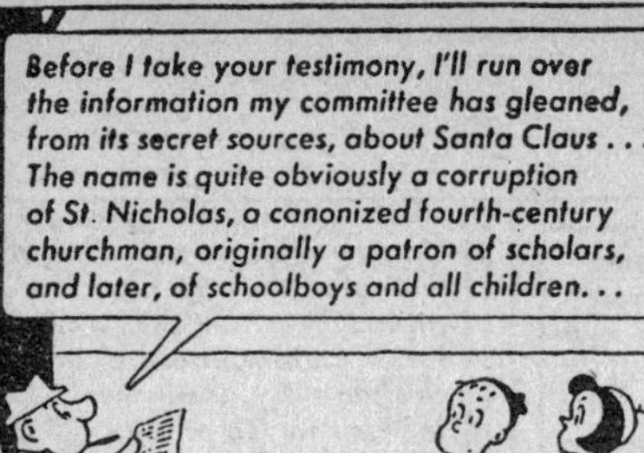
Before I take your testimony, I'll run over the information my committee has gleaned, from its secret sources, about Santa Claus . . . The name is quite obviously a corruption of St. Nicholas, a canonized fourth-century churchman, originally a patron of scholars, and later, of schoolboys and all children. . .
11-29

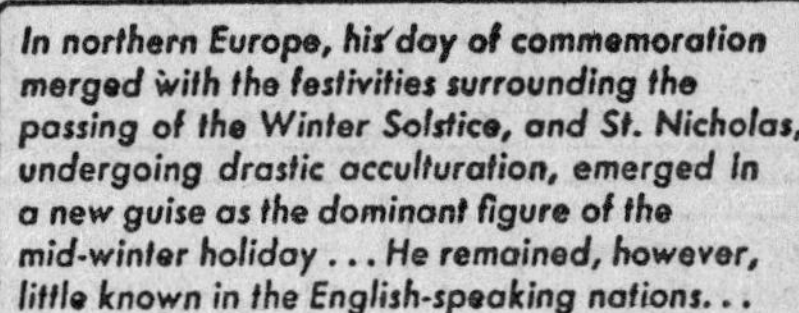
In northern Europe, his day of commemoration merged with the festivities surrounding the passing of the Winter Solstice, and St. Nicholas, undergoing drastic acculturation, emerged in a new guise as the dominant figure of the mid-winter holiday . . . He remained, however, little known in the English-speaking nations. . .
Copyright 1943 Field Publications
CROCKETT JOHNSON

In England, it was not until Queen Victoria's marriage to Albert, and, in America, not until German immigration near the middle of the nineteenth century, that either country—
Gosh, Mr. O'Malley, Pop will be sore about that page getting torn out of our encyclopedia.

The O'Malley Committee seeks merely to learn the truth about Santa Claus, m'boy. Is he a myth masquerading as a man? . . . Or vice versa? . . . Either way, he won't look good in headlines.
Then my unbiased committee will find out whether this Claus is a rogue taking fraudulent credit for the Christmas benevolence you children enjoy, or whether he IS to blame for this practice which spoils and softens up our youth.
In my first preliminary reports to the press, I'll—
Gosh, Mr. O'Malley. When you finish investigating him, Santa Claus won't—
Barnaby! We mustn't prejudge things. This investigation is to be conducted in a fair and impartial manner.
CROCKETT JOHNSON
Copyright 1943 Field Publications

Now suppose you give a detailed description of Santa Claus for our investigating committee files. You observed him closely, I trust. What unusual characteristics has he? . . .
There wasn't anything unusual about him . . .
12-1

Come. I'm afraid you're not a very observant pair of investigators—
He had on a red suit, Mr. O'Malley, with a pillow stuffed in it . . .

And bushy white false whiskers—
False whiskers! Cushlamochree! . . . I apologize—

Copyright 1943 Field Publications
CROCKETT JOHNSON
It was a clever piece of work recognizing him at all! In that DISGUISE!
But—

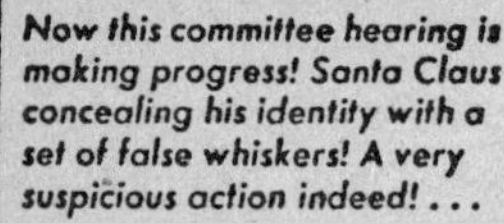
Now this committee hearing is making progress! Santa Claus concealing his identity with a set of false whiskers! A very suspicious action indeed! . . .

But—
He ALWAYS wears them.
12·2

You mean he makes a HABIT of going about in a red suit with a pillow in it and an artificial beard? And people take him for granted? This surely proves the crying need for my investigation!

A mythical upstart! Flaunting his acceptance into our culture! But the constabulary—surely it has questioned this outlandish character, with no job, and no visible means of support, who—
He's got a job . . .

Copyright 1943 Field Publications
CROCKETT JOHNSON
Sure, Mr. O'Malley. The department store . . . He works there every year.

If there was some way to catch this Claus fellow off guard! To have him incriminate himself . . . You've both seen him and spoken to him. Are you and he on fairly good terms?
Oh, sure, Mr. O'Malley.
He even patted me on the head . . . And I didn't holler like most of the kids . . .
12-3
Excellent! Because as secret operatives for the O'Malley Committee to Investigate Santa Claus you may have to contact him again!
CROCKETT JOHNSON
Copyright 1943 Field Publications
I'll devise some clever pretext for you and your mothers to visit the toy section of the department store. Let's see—

Hey, Mom. Will you take me to see Santa Claus so I can talk to him?
Why—yes, Barnaby. Of course.
12-4

I didn't think he believed in Santa Claus any more . . .
Jane never has. I've had to persuade her to take any interest at all in him, and—

Ma! You won't forget to take me to see Santa Claus this year, will you?
What IS this?
CROCKETT JOHNSON

It's no trouble, Mr. O'Malley . . . We'd have gone to see Santa Claus anyway . . . We wouldn't spoil all our mothers' fun . . .
Copyright 1943 Field Publications

Mr. O'Malley! Jane's mother isn't going with us to see Santa Claus tomorrow. She has a cold . . . But my mother will take Jane and me.
Too bad about Mrs. Shultz, m'boy. . . . We need all our operatives to insure the success of my plan to beard this Claus in his den . . . But we'll manage, won't we, Gus?
12-6
Me? Go Into a department store? During the Christmas rush? Even the January white sale leaves me haggard!... No, O'Malley, NO!
Very well. We'll carry on without you, too, Gus . . .
I hope your mother won't lose heart when she learns of this further depletion of our party.
Barnaby, does your mother know HE's coming with us? . . .

I'll fly in a window and we'll all meet—er—at the lunch counter. . . . Now . . . How can we get YOU into the store inconspicuously? Don't want this Claus forewarned. . . . Lose the element of surprise.
12-7

With my makeup artistry and all the stuff in this attic—Ah! These sunglasses . . . And a hat and veil! And a bit of this bathrobe cord frayed up to make a mustache . . . Nobody will recognize you as a pair of special investigators . . .

Mom. Mr. O'Malley fixed it so Santa Claus won't know us
Barnaby, that's silly. How could that imaginary pixie possibly—

Copyright 1943 Field Publications

Mom. We have to find my Fairy Godfather, Mr. O'Malley. He's—
We'll never find an imaginary pixie in this crowded store, son.
12-8
He'll be easy to find, Mom. He's disguised.
UP
Look! . . . On the down escalator! It's Mr. O'Malley!
CROCKETT JOHNSON
Copyright 1943 Field Publications

Now keep very close together—
Jane! Where did Barnaby go?
Down on that other escalator . . . He saw his Fairy Godfather.
12 9
Copyright 1943 Field Publications
It's impossible! Finding Barnaby in this crowd! Anyone HIS size—
CROCKETT JOHNSON
Look, Stella. A midget . . . Dressed up funny. From the toy section—
He's supposed to be a gnome or something.
Cushlamochree! Gnome, indeed! I, madam, am a—
Mr. O'Malley!

There's a play pen for lost tots, madam, in the toy department—
What do you think of kids that get lost, Mrs. Baxter?
12-10
Of course, maybe they can't help getting lost. . . . If they haven't got very intelligent IQs . . .
He's not here. I wonder if—while I make another search—you'd mind—
Bright kids never wind up in places like this though—
CROCKETT JOHNSON
Copyright 1943 Field Publications
Lost Children
HEY!

Gosh, Mr. O'Malley. I don't know where Mom and Jane are . . . They must be LOST.
Look, m'boy! . . . This grasping institution even does a business in Lost Children! Cushlamochree! They don't miss a trick—
12-11
CROCKETT JOHNSON
Lost Children
Jane!
Copyright 1943 Field Publications
Put a small deposit on her, Barnaby, and wait here for me . . . I'll look around for the Lost Parents Department . . .

12-13
Lost Children
Get me out of here!
THERE you are!
Mr. O'Malley just left to—
Nonsense. A little man with wings! In a crowded store!
He said to wait—
A fine commotion he'd cause if he really was here, Barnaby.
It's funny he hasn't caused a commotion.
Yet.
CROCKETT JOHNSON
CRASH!
CUSHLAMOCHREE!
Mom! There he is! At the construction toy counter!

12-14
That construction toy display fell down. An accident. Your imaginary elf had nothing to do with it! . . . He doesn't exist!
Mr. O'Malley isn't an elf—
I want to make a complaint! That midget you have driving around in that kiddie jeep—
He ran over my foot—
CROCKETT JOHNSON
Copyright 1943 Field Publications
A fat little dwarf demonstrating the chemical sets! He poured—
Dwarf? We have no dwarf, madam.
Whaaah!
SECTION MANAGER

All right! Maybe it WAS your Fairy Godfather who caused all those accidents, Barnaby . . . We'll not argue about it . . . Now go see Santa Claus. And we'll hope there won't be any more trouble.
But Mr. O'Malley wouldn't cause any trouble on purpose, Mom.
Copyright 1943 Field Publications 12-15
No, of course not, but—
We'll be right back. We just have to pull Santa's whiskers off.
WHAT?—JANE!—BARNABY!
But Mr. O'Malley told us to, Mom—
CROCKETT JOHNSON

Your mother said not to pull his whiskers off, Barnaby . . .
But Mr. O'Malley told us to beard him in his lair—
12-16

Well, why doesn't your Fairy Godfather do it himself if—
Maybe he will—Look!

Isn't that Mr. O'Malley? Near that counter full of real model airplanes?
Copyright 1943 Field Publications

It must be him!
CROCKETT JOHNSON

12·17
Here comes another one!
Imagine that, Barnaby! His beard is REAL!
CROCKETT JOHNSON

Someone wound up all the model airplanes!
Help!
Police!
Goodness! This way, children!
Are we going to the air raid shelter?
12-18
A BIG one! It flew out the window!
CRASH!
Cushlamochree!
Copyright 1943 Field Publications
Mom! That was Mr. O'Malley, my Fairy Godfather!
CROCKETT JOHNSON

Those crowds in that department store! Rioting! Jarring my sensitive nerves! . . . I expected the place to be completely deserted! Everyone was urged to shop early! Shouldn't have been one single soul in the store! . . . It was all a plot of that Claus, with his phony whiskers, to—
Did you tell your Fairy Godfather Santa Claus' whiskers are REAL?
12 20
Copyright 1943 Field Publications
What? Claus has real whiskers? Cushlamochree! . . . Is it possible my investigation of him has been proceeding on a wrong tack? . . . Many of these folk legends HAVE a basis in fact, you know, and—
CROCKETT JOHNSON
I must mull over this information, m'boy . . .
He sounds like he might get to believe in Santa Claus, Barnaby.

12-21
Gosh. You have your earmuffs on, Mr. O'Malley.
Yes, of course. It's winter now . . . Barnaby, on this Santa Claus matter. I have a clever idea for laying any doubts we may have that the beneficence attributed to him is specious . . .

We'll write him a letter. In your name. Requesting that, among the usual run-of-the-mill toys, he bring one specific present—say—a set of boxing gloves . . .
Okay . . . But I don't think it will work.

Very likely not. In which case I can confidently denounce him as a fraud . . . But if, by chance, the gloves DO arrive—well, we have a set of boxing gloves . . .
Copyright 1943 Field Publications
CROCKETT JOHNSON

When those boxing gloves arrive, Barnaby, I'll show you a trick I taught Kid McCoy. The shoelace gag. Sports columnists still write about it on rainy days. . .
12 22
McCoy worked it beautifully. He brought over a hard left, stunning his opponent. Then while he was still dazed, the Kid quickly tied the poor chap's shoelaces together and—But I can't explain the rest of it until those boxing gloves—
Do you really think Santa Claus will bring them, Mr. O'Malley?
Eh? Oh, I mean IF he were to bring them . . . If there WAS a Santa Claus who did things like that, Barnaby . . .
CROCKETT JOHNSON
Of course, I don't really believe it—
Say, m'boy. What are the inside measurements of this fireplace chimney?

It's funny how everybody gets to believe in Santa Claus bringing presents this time of year, Barnaby.
The grownups seem to. Maybe we're too young to believe in him, Jane.
12·23

Even your Fairy Godfather—
Mr. O'Malley? Well, he doesn't REALLY believe in Santa—
Listen!
Cushlamochree!

CROCKETT JOHNSON
Gosh! He's stuck!

Difficult. But it CAN be done.
But Mr. O'Malley. . . . Santa Claus is bigger than you.

Christmas Eve! An opportunity to solve this Santa Claus mystery once and for all . . . I'll cleverly conceal myself in your living room, keeping a constant vigil!
Okay, Mr. O'Malley. Too bad I have to go to bed now . . . It's eight o'clock.
12-24
Almost midnight. I guess we're all set. Let's wake Barnaby . . .
This is one time we can take his mind off that imaginary little pixie—
OH, BARNABY! —SANTA HAS BEEN HERE!—
CROCKETT JOHNSON
But where's Mr. O'Malley?

This just arrived from Aunt Emma. I'll slip it under the tree. Barnaby will think he overlooked it when he opened the other presents last night . . . Aunt Emma's gifts are never exciting anyway . . . Woolen underwear or maybe overshoes—
Barnaby is coming down now.
12-25

Mr. O'Malley! Gosh! Were you behind that couch all night?
Santa's been here? I must have dozed—

I don't think it was Santa Claus. The only thing we asked HIM for isn't here—the boxing gloves—
Here's a package you missed, m'boy.

CROCKETT JOHNSON
Copyright 1943 Field Publications
Look, Barnaby! Good old Santa!

CROCKETT JOHNSON
Is that what was in that package from Aunt Emma, Barnaby? Boxing gloves?
Aunt Emma sent them?
Copyright 1943 Field Publications
12-27

Mr. O'Malley! Aunt Emma gave me the boxing gloves. It wasn't Santa Claus . . . So you'll have to keep on investigating him, huh?
Aunt Emma?

Public interest in Santa Claus is at low ebb after Christmas, m'boy. My startling revelations won't get the headlines they deserve . . . So my committee ought perhaps turn its attention toward something else Say! How about the Easter Bunny?
When is Easter?

Same day as usual. First Sunday after the first full moon after the Vernal Equinox . . . But that's some time away, isn't it m'boy?
While we're waiting, let's slip on the boxing gloves and go a few fast rounds.

Can I box in the living room?
No, Barnaby—who were you going to box with, anyway?
12-28

Mr. O'Malley, my Fairy Godfather.
It's no fun sparring with an imaginary pixie, son. Let's you and I put on a bout.

We'll get the gloves and take them down the cellar where we can really cut loose.
Will you box Mr. O'Malley, too, Pop? . . .

CROCKETT JOHNSON
Mr. O'Malley's gone!
And so are the boxing gloves!

If you want me to box with you, son, you'll have to recall what you did with the gloves. Did you take them upstairs?
No.
12·29

Well where did you leave them? They're not in your room. . . In the cellar? On the porch? Outdoors?
Mr. O'Malley, my Fairy Godfather, must have taken them away, Pop.

Nonsense!
But, Pop—

John. I thought you promised Barnaby you'd box with him.
Mr. O'Malley took the boxing gloves.
CROCKETT JOHNSON

Returning your boxing gloves, m'boy. They've been used in an elimination tournament held to determine the champion of the Elves, Leprechauns, Gnomes and Little Men's Chowder and Marching Society . . . A fiasco . . .
12-30 Copyright 1943 Field Publications
You won't believe this . . . The Society's new champion is LAUNCELOT McSNOYD!
That little leprechaun?
I couldn't believe it, either, when they told me about it—
When they TOLD you? But didn't you see him win? Didn't you box in the tournament?
Before it began, I was prevailed upon to engage in an exhibition bout. With a sturdy elf. And, er—
Gosh, Mr. O'Malley! Look at your EYE!
CROCKETT JOHNSON

Want to box, Mr. O'Malley?
No! Er, not now, m'boy. I'm working on several monumental pieces of legislation I must put up to Congress Monday.
12-31
I want to get there early to attach these Riders to all the bills on the floor. Don't want to be seen in the House with this black eye. The fellows are such kidders, you know—
I guess I'll make a snowman. Then I can box with HIM . . .
. . . "Amendment to an amendment to revise a revision of"—What?
A snowman?
Box with a snowman? An excellent idea! I'll come along too. After all, m'boy, "All work and no play—"
CROCKETT JOHNSON

Pop! My Fairy Godfather is boxing with a snowman.
Tell Mr. O'Malley to keep his left up, son.
Don't give him ideas.
Fitzsimmons couldn't get it. . . . I kept demonstrating it for him. "This way, Bob—"
CROCKETT JOHNSON
Pop! . . . The snowman! . . . He knocked out Mr. O'Malley!

Joe Snodgrass goes into the Army Friday . . . I may be called any day now—
Army routine will be hard, won't it? On men your age—
My age! Why I'm in fine shape—
All that marching— And you wrenched a thigh running after Barnaby's football—
Nonsense . . . All I need is a bit of limbering up . . . Mightn't be a bad idea to get hold of a set of Indian clubs. I'll call the sporting goods store . . .
. . . And chest weights . . . And a punching bag . . . What? A rowing machine? Yes, send one over . . . And parallel bars—
Copyright 1944 Field Publications
CROCKETT JOHNSON

This seems like an awful lot of equipment just to take a few exercises on—
I'll be using it all, getting in shape . . . And another thing: A gym like this will keep Barnaby so occupied he'll stop imagining visits from his "Fairy Godfather" . . . It's worth a lot, isn't it, to keep that pixie away from here?
1-4
Come and look, Mr. O'Malley.
I was just leaving for Washington—
CROCKETT JOHNSON
Cushlamochree! Very interesting indeed! . . . I shall postpone my departure a few days.

The workout I'm taking in our "gym" every morning really is making me feel worlds better. Everybody ought to get some regular exercise nowadays . . .
Congressmen, too, Pop? . . .
Congressmen? Of course. Why not? . . . As a matter of fact, the congressional physician claims they're all overworked and don't get enough exercise . . . He also says they need a month's rest—
Huh?
CROCKETT JOHNSON
Mr. O'Malley! . . . The doctor in Congress said you need a whole month's vacation! . . .
Be careful, O'Malley.
A month off? And doctor's orders! Can't ignore THAT, can I, m'boy?

Yes, work in Congress is extremely exhausting. Especially on the Useless Papers Committee . . . The way they've allowed things to accumulate! Imagine! Saving receipts from the Louisiana Purchase . . . As though we could get our money back if we were dissatisfied . . . Furthermore—
Pop says the doc in Congress said Congressmen also need exercise . . . Long walks and—
Somebody might fall over these, O'Malley.
1-6
Copyright 1944 Field Publications
Long walks? . . . I don't think I see eye to eye with him there, m'boy.
Might be therapeutically sound, but POLITICALLY— Well, m'boy. where is Al Smith, today? . . . Running an observation tower! . . .
CROCKETT JOHNSON

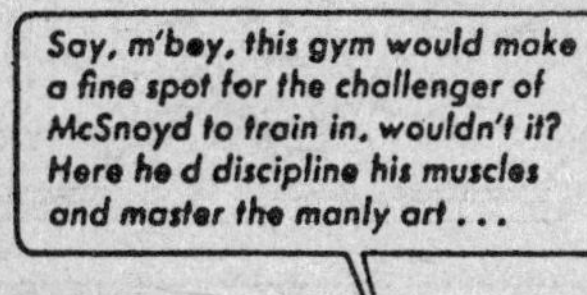

Say, m'bey, this gym would make a fine spot for the challenger of McSnoyd to train in, wouldn't it? Here he d discipline his muscles and master the manly art . . .

A gladiator who will wrench the championship crown of the Elves, Leprechauns, Gnomes, and Little Men's Society from the unworthy brow of that ridiculous little leprechaun!
You?

No, not me, m'boy. But I'd like to take a likely youngster in hand and develop him. Give him the benefit of my vast ring lore . . . Where can I find a suitable prospect . . . AH!

CROCKETT JOHNSON
No, O'Malley—NO!

Hello, m'boy. The articles are all signed for the big bout . . . . Gus, the Ghost versus McSnoyd, the Leprechaun! . . . Gus has started intensive training . . .
1-8

Lucky, isn't he, having a tutor of my long experience in the squared circle . . . Ever see this photo of me, Barnaby? John L. O'Malley, the Boston Strong Boy.
You had a mustache!

Yes . . . I shaved it off . . . People kept mistaking me for Tyrone Power . . . Steady now, Gus. I'm going to increase the beat . . .
But, O'Malley—

Copyright 1944 Field Publications
CROCKETT JOHNSON
This won't be so hard tomorrow, Gus . . . If I can get hold of an outboard motor . . .

Copyright 1944 Field Publications
Mr. O'Malley, will it be fair for Gus to box that leprechaun? He's about this big, isn't he? And—
Yes . . . He's rather tall—for a leprechaun. And he's wiry, too. Very wiry. Weighs about two and a half pounds—
1-10
Cushlamochree! I hadn't thought of it, m'boy! . . . The discrepancy in the weight of the two opponents!
Gus! Hop on these scales!
Two and a half pounds!
Yes. McSnoyd HAS the advantage.
Gosh! Gus doesn't weigh ANYTHING!
CROCKETT JOHNSON

That leprechaun outweighs you by a mere two and a half pounds, Gus. That's nothing to the weight Dempsey gave away to Willard—
But Gus weighs nothing at all!

About average for a ghost. A good training diet will build him up a bit, too . . . I'll speak to your mother about it, m'boy.
Meanwhile, do some shadow boxing, Gus.
But, O'Malley—
Copyright 1944 Field Publications

I know, I know, Gus. You haven't GOT a shadow . . . Just imagine you have one. Until I work something out . . . Oh, the problems a manager must cope with! And for a measly third of the purse! Come, m'boy. First I'll plan the week's menus . . .
Gus has no shadow?
CROCKETT JOHNSON

Mom! Mr. O'Malley, my Fairy Godfather, wants to tell you how to cook. Gus, the Ghost, is training for a fight and—
Your mother can become another Madame Bey . . .
12

In a few months the house will be full of boxfighters—
What's this? On the stove?
MOM! . . . She's out.

Copyright 1944 Field Publications
Hmm . . . Soy beans. Too bad she didn't consult me about this dish, m'boy . . .

She'd have been surprised and delighted to learn of a much more easily prepared substitute, containing most of the nutritional values of soy beans, too . . . A two-inch cut of T-bone sirloin steak.
CROCKETT JOHNSON

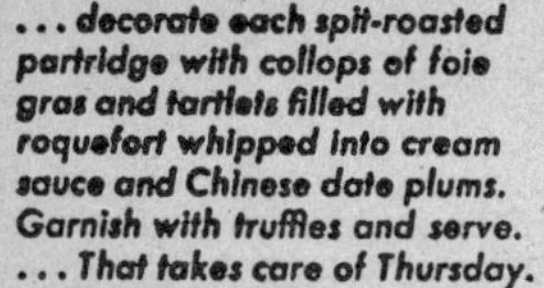
. . . decorate each spit-roasted partridge with collops of foie gras and tartlets filled with roquefort whipped into cream sauce and Chinese date plums. Garnish with truffles and serve. . . . That takes care of Thursday.

1-13

Your folks may begin to tire of all this hearty peasant fare, so Friday's menu will be something really special! The creation that catapulted the name "O'Malley of the Waldorf" to the highest pinnacle of the culinary arts . . .

What a sensation when it first appeared on the carte du jour! Père Delmonico hurried over to clasp my hand! Old man Rector sulked! "Why," they heard him mutter, "didn't I think of it?"—
What was it, Mr. O'Malley?
CROCKETT JOHNSON

Copyright 1944 Field Publications
Meat and potatoes!

. . . a ten-pound prime rib roast—garnished, of course, with truffles—and mashed potatoes. Whip the two potatoes in a quart of heavy cream and a pound of butter and—
Mr.O'Malley, won't these meals cost Mom a lot?
1-14
Copyright 1944 Field Publications
No . . . You see, the next day's menu is made up entirely of LEFTOVERS . . . Your mother will understand how that keeps everything within the budget.
Leftovers?
Yes . . . Take five or six pounds of leftover filet mignon, broil slightly—saves fuel too, you see—and serve with a sauce made of three leftover young female lobsters, diced, leftover chestnuts, leftover madeira . . .
and, er, oh yes—slices of leftover truffles—Er, say, m'boy, I've got an appetite! How about a few of these fine nourishing soy beans?
CROCKETT JOHNSON

"Gentleman Jim O'Malley," they used to ask me, "to what do you attribute your unrivaled prowess in the manly art of self-defense?" . . . And I'd set down my glass and cigar and pool cue and say, "Clean living and ROADWORK!" . . . So—
1-15 Copyright 1944 Field Publications

But, O'Malley! Around the reservoir? It's five miles!
Now you run with Gus and keep him company. Don't go chasing laundry wagons or—
Where could I find a laundry wagon?

CROCKETT JOHNSON
Well, they're off at last, m'boy. Sometimes I think Gus wasn't cut out to be a fighter . . . But the sport has to be kept alive. . . . With the best we have left. Until Joe Louis comes back . . .

Gus should enjoy his roadwork . . . A brisk five-mile jaunt around the reservoir and through the woods, with a faithful dog trotting along beside him, happily and contentedly—
Mr. O'Malley! Look! Gorgon ran away from Gus. He's chasing another truck!
WET WASH
LAUNDRY

That dog! After we told him to stick close to Gus! . . . What disobedience! . . . It's a lack of proper training. Some day I'll—
The truck's stopped. The man's gone into Mrs. Jones' house—
CROCKETT
JOHNSON

Achoo!
GUS!
WET
WASH

O'Malley—Achoo!—I got half way around the reservoir to that brook near the—Aachoo!
Only halfway? Well, you got up a good sweat—
1-18
CROCKETT JOHNSON

My training regimen is building you up wonderfully, Gus. You've gained over a pound already—
But—Achoo!
Maybe it's because he's sopping wet.

O'Malley! Listen! The brook! The dam has burst! That end of the woods is inundated and I fell in! It's a FLOOD! An awful disaster!
But nobody lives down there, Gus—

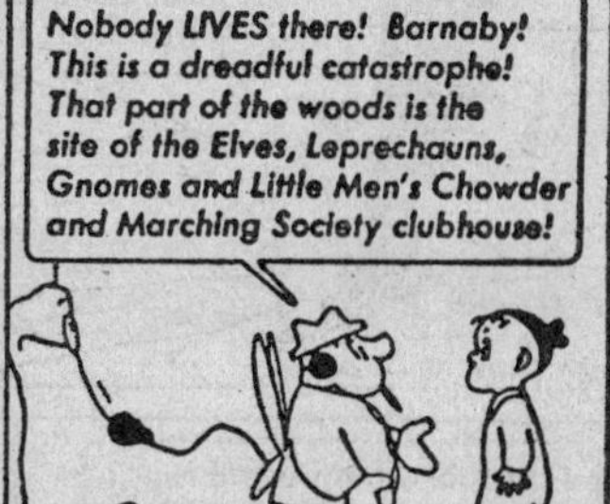
Nobody LIVES there! Barnaby! This is a dreadful catastrophe! That part of the woods is the site of the Elves, Leprechauns, Gnomes and Little Men's Chowder and Marching Society clubhouse!

Gus, we must visit the scene of this calamitous flood. I'll direct the rescue work and speak a few words before the newsreel cameras. . . . I imagine the wire services will want a few pictures, too. "Congressman O'Malley Aids Disaster Victims". . .
The boxing match! It will be cancelled now, O'Malley, won't it? . . .
1-19 Copyright 1944 Field Publications
"O'Malley Carries Wood Nymph to Safety". . . "Comforts Homeless Elves". . . And that sort of thing.
The fight! Is it off?
CROCKETT JOHNSON
The fight OFF? It's more important than ever! . . . Part of the proceeds will go to the O'Malley Fund to Aid Flood Sufferers!
Oh, dear.

They've given me a big job at the plant . . . We've got to prove to the government that the proposed dam for the river must be built at once. I'm to put all the data on the town's war industries together in a convincing argument . . . I may have to go to Washington. . . We've had no help from our congressman . . . Can't even find him—
You can't find Mr. O'Malley, Pop? My Fairy Godfather?... I'll get him—
Copyright 1944 Field Publications
Hush, Barnaby. . . Yes. This fellow O'Malley we elected to Congress doesn't answer letters or wires—
He's been very busy—
BARNABY! GO TO BED!
But I'll get him to build the dam for you, Pop. If you tell me the kind you want—
CROCKETT JOHNSON

Mr. O'Malley, my Fairy Godfather, has been busy training Gus the Ghost for the fight he's going to have with a leprechaun. And now he's out rescuing the elves and gnomes that live in the woods where the brook overflowed . . .
1-21
But if Pop's company wants a dam built on the river, Mr. O'Malley could find time to—
Goodnight, Barnaby.
Hello, m'boy. Can't stay but a minute! I've made a thorough inspection of the flood area. Freezing weather temporarily has arrested the surge of the waters. Must get back there.
CROCKETT JOHNSON
I dropped in to borrow these. I am giving a figure skating exhibition in the ballroom of the Elves, Leprechauns, Gnomes and Little Men's Clubhouse . . .

I've assured all my colleagues at the Elves, Leprechauns, Gnomes, and Little Men's Chowder and Marching Society that there's no danger from that burst dam in the brook . . . As long as this freezing weather holds out . . .
1 22

I'll think of a solution to the problem before the spring thaw sets in . . . I'm responsible, in a way, for this mishap. It seems I antagonized the beavers. And they moved away, abandoning the maintenance of their dam.
Beavers?
CROCKETT JOHNSON
Congress! Why didn't I think of it, m'boy! . . . I'll have Congress approve a gigantic engineering project for that brook!
"THE O'MALLEY DAM"!
Copyright 1944 Field Publications

Yes . . . One day I happened to be mulling over the question of riparian rights, and I, er—
Pop wants Congress to build a BIG dam, Mr. O'Malley, and—

Keep that up for a few hours, Gus . . . Until I work out plans of the big O'Malley Dam for Congress to approve. I want to submit complete blueprints—
Are YOU going to make the plans, Mr. O'Malley? Did you ever make any?
1-24 Copyright 1944 Field Publications

Barnaby, your Fairy Godfather has designed the most talked about dams in the country. All of them have been sensational! . . . Williamsburg . . . The South Fork Dam above Johnstown . . .
. . . Walnut Grove, in Arizona . . . Austin . . . The St. Francis Dam in California . . . Oh, they didn't all turn out to be sensational right away. It took several of them years to make the front pages . . .
Gosh.
CROCKETT JOHNSON

Training Gus and designing a huge dam project at the same time is nothing . . . With MY capacity for work.
1-25

Luckily, I'm both a mathematical genius and a— Mmm! 684÷23! Cushlamochree! Long Division!
Copyright 1944 Field Publications

On second thought, Barnaby, I'm needlessly taxing my energy . . . With my executive ability, I can relegate some of these chores . . . Suppose YOU keep an eye on Gus. And I'll get that dam designed . . .

CROCKETT JOHNSON
I know just the person to do it, too! . . . What's at the movies today, m'boy?

Mr. O'Malley! Gus stopped punching the bag . . . He fell asleep again, Mr. O'Malley—
Eh? Hello, m'boy.
1-26

I guess that's all right. We don't want him trained too fine anyway . . . Can't afford to have him lose his edge before he climbs into the ring with that leprechaun.
Copyright 1944 Field Publications

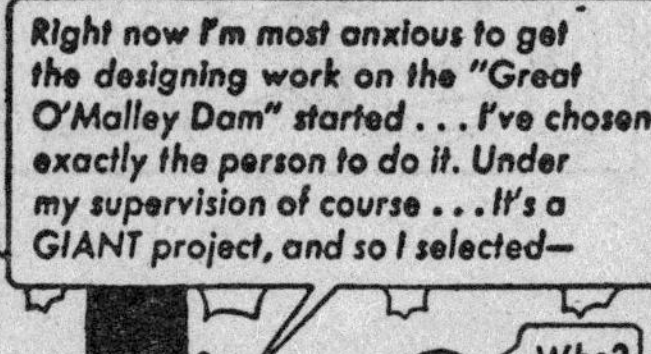
Right now I'm most anxious to get the designing work on the "Great O'Malley Dam" started . . . I've chosen exactly the person to do it. Under my supervision of course . . . It's a GIANT project, and so I selected—

Who?
CROCKETT JOHNSON

A Giant. Naturally. My old friend, Atlas, the Mental Giant.
?

Gosh. The Mental Giant doesn't remember you, Mr. O'Malley . . .
He'll recall who I am in a moment, m'boy . . . Atlas NEVER forgets He has a system . . .
1-27

He doesn't weigh down his mind with countless complex series of vowels and consonants. Instead of a person's name he remembers a simple mathematical formula—
$(e^{\pi i}+1)+M\int_0^A dx+\begin{vmatrix}\log N & y \\ -In^{-1} & L^2\end{vmatrix}_{N\to 10}$

Isn't that harder to remember?
Not for Atlas. He's a Mental Giant . . . Then he works it out like that. On his slide rule.
O + MA + LL + EY

CROCKETT JOHNSON
See, m'boy? A sure fire scientific memory aid.
O'Malley!

Atlas, old pal, I'm here to offer you the opportunity of working on the design of the mammoth O'Malley Dam, the erection of which will begin as soon as I get Congress' approval. A gigantic multiple-arch structure with several diversion tunnels which can be used as pen-stocks and spillway conduits and—
A difficult undertaking, O'Malley . . .
CROCKETT JOHNSON
1-28
Copyright 1944 Field Publications
Of course it's a big job. I wouldn't entrust it to ANYone . . . But a Mental Giant of your caliber—
How wide is the river?
It's a brook—
Hush, Barnaby . . . About 997 millimeters, approximately . . .
Mmm. More than three feet! . . . Mmm. It IS a difficult undertaking!

Mr. O'Malley, I have to go home—
Yes, yes. But I've got to tell Atlas the requirements of this project . . .
1-29
I don't think sluice gates will be practical, Atlas. I prefer huge electrically operated needle valves—
Gosh.
Copyright 1944 Field Publications
Gosh. A Fairy Godfather with a magic wand and a Mental Giant should be able to figure out a dam for a little brook three feet wide pretty easily—
The small stream presents our big difficulty, m'boy. We must widen it.
Or the dam won't be big enough to hold those colossal twin statues of O'Malley.
CROCKETT JOHNSON

Well, Gus, the great O'Malley Dam project is under way. The important features are all worked out . . . One of the twin colossal statues of me will face upstream. In sort of a King Canute pose. And the other—
Atlas, the Mental Giant, is going to help on the dam—
But, O'Malley. Will it be built in time? . . . Before the thaws and Spring floods?
1-31 Copyright 1948 Field Publications
Of course! . . . Construction will start immediately! As soon as Congress acts on the proposal! And I'm submitting it at once! The instant detailed plans and specifications are completed!
When will that be?
CROCKETT JOHNSON
They'll be drawn up without a moment's delay. Right after Atlas finishes the preliminary design. And he's beginning on his rough draft any day now.

I don't want to rush any of the work on the O'Malley Dam unnecessarily . . . Just want it completed before the Spring floods . . . With my knowledge of meteorology I can establish exactly when warm weather will set in this year. Remind me to do that, m'boy. Tomorrow.
How will you do it, O'Malley?
I'll remind you Mr. O'Malley . . .
2-1
Copyright 1944 Field Publications

By a method I persuaded the Weather Bureau to adopt a while back. It's very simple.
How does it work? By magic?
It's merely an application of the usual procedure of exact scientific observation—to a Ground Hog and his shadow.
CROCKETT JOHNSON

The advent of Spring will be retarded if the Ground Hog sees his shadow and retreats into his hole. I'm not entirely clear on the meteorological theory involved, m'boy, but—
Maybe he's afraid of his shadow.
2·2
I doubt if unreal horrors affect the behavior of so unimaginative an animal—
Here he comes, Mr. O'Malley!
Copyright 1944 Field Publications
CROCKETT JOHNSON
He didn't see his shadow, Mr. O'Malley. He saw you!

Barnaby, another difficulty . . . Atlas informs me that before he can begin the plan of the great O'Malley Dam we must make a topographic, a geologic, and a hydrographic survey . . .
2-3
I'll run over to the brook and make them now. I dropped in to borrow an engineer's level, a transit, an odometer, and—
Gosh. We haven't got any, Mr. O'Malley . . .
Rather poorly equipped household . . . However, I'll manage with a prismatic compass, a theodolite, a sextant, a cyclometer—
But—
Copyright 1944 Field Publications
Cushlamochree . . . Well, at least, there's a TAPE MEASURE . . . Here in your mother's sewing basket.

While Gus and I are surveying the site of the O'Malley Dam, we'll ferret out the location of McSnoyd's secret quarters—
Don't you know where he is?
2-9
No. Our unscrupulous opponent made himself invisible . . . And he's gone off somewhere . . . No doubt to devise some new foul punch . . . Away from the raised eyebrows of true sport lovers.
CROCKETT JOHNSON
But, invisible or not, that leprechaun won't conceal his whereabouts from ME—
Cushlamochree!
Copyright 1944 Field Publications
Barnaby! . . . Throwing snowballs! . . . At your old Fairy Godfather!
Dear me!
Huh?

Barnaby, that dopey ghost is still practicing how to box in your cellar, isn't he?
Oh, hello, Jane.
2-3
Gus and Mr. O'Malley, my Fairy Godfather, went to search for the secret place the invisible leprechaun is training in . . . So Gus isn't there right now, but—
He's not?
Well, who's punching the punching bag?
Nobody. Nobody's home . . .
CROCKETT JOHNSON
Copyright 1944 Field Publications
ThudThudThud
THUD
THUD
ThudThud!

My Fairy Godfather, Mr. O'Malley, and Gus the Ghost are out trying to find the invisible leprechaun's secret training camp . . . So there can't be anybody in the cellar . . .
2-7
See. Nobody's here. Maybe we imagined we heard the punching bag.
Copyright 1944 Field Publications
I didn't imagine it—Where did you say the invisible leprechaun was training?
CROCKETT JOHNSON
That's what Mr. O'Malley is going to find out . . .

2-8
I'm glad that punching bag is taking our son's attention away from those imaginary pixies and things he says hang around our house. But ask him to lay off awhile . . .
THUD THUD!
ThudThudThud!
Until I check these estimates on that proposed river dam . . .
I'll call to him. I think Jane is down there, too.
CROCKETT JOHNSON
Thud
Thud
Thud!
Barnaby! Jane! Go outdoors and play for a while.
Copyright 1944 Field Publications
And when my Fairy Godfather finds out where the invisible leprechaun is training, he—
Listen, Barnaby . . . I think that's your mother calling us.

Well, m'boy, we've scoured the woods! Not a sign of the invisible leprechaun's secret training quarters!
Gosh.
2-9
O'Malley, do you think he may have—er—run out? . . . That my commitment to the contest is abrogated?
You're unduly alarmed, Gus.
After all, McSnoyd has no way of knowing what great fighting shape you're in . . . These training quarters of YOURS are secret too, Gus.
CROCKETT JOHNSON
I'll moider the bum!
Horrors!
McSnoyd!
Copyright 1944 Field Publications

Help! He uttered a homicidal threat!
McSnoyd! Have you no sense of propriety? Working out in your opponent's secret camp!
O'Malley! . . . Me pal!
Pop! . . . There's an invisible leprechaun in our cellar! . . . He sneaked in!
Copyright 1944 Field Publications
2-10
Pop won't believe it, Mr. O'Malley.
So your old man doubts your woid? Send O'Malley up to confoim it, kid.
CROCKETT JOHNSON
Of course your father won't believe it, m'boy. Nobody will believe such bad manners can exist! But don't bother your dad further. I'll handle this.
Hoid any good ones, O'Malley?

Get out of our cellar, you invisible old leprechaun!
Okay, kid. I was on the voige of showing O'Malley the secret punch I poifected, but—
Eh? Well, McSnoyd, suppose you demonstrate it. If I consider it not up to Boxing's severe ethical standards, I'll file a complaint with the NBA . . . Not that Gus and I are a bit worried about it. . .
2-11
Copyright 1944 Field Publications
Watch close, O'Malley. . . . Foist I feint like this . . . Then I step in—
But I can't see—
Be careful, Mr. O'Malley!
CROCKETT JOHNSON
Hey!

Gus has nothing to fear, Barnaby. McSneyd's secret sneak punch is nothing but a roundhouse right! He won't be able to land it when Gus can see him.
That there was a left hook, O'Malley.
2-12
And of course he'll have to make himself visible the night of the contest. So—
Foist I hold of it, pal. It ain't in the agreement.
O'Malley, that White Hope of yours—in the toise voinacular of the late Joe Jacobs—"should of stood in bed." With the other sheets . . . Tell the spook I'll be seeing him. In the old squared coicle. Too bad he won't see me.
But—
Copyright 1944 Field Publications
Gus has to box that leprechaun even if he can't see him? Gosh!
Bad habit of mine, isn't it, Gus? Signing things without reading them—SAY! . . . Where IS Gus?
CROCKETT JOHNSON

Gus . . . After—er—observing your adversary in action, I'm afraid we must—er—revise our tactics—
Don't worry, O'Malley.
Huh?
2-14

In addition to a somewhat unorthodox stance, he—er—
It can't bother me.
Gus isn't scared!

CROC JOHN
He's going to be INVISIBLE through the whole fight!
It doesn't matter.
What?

KETT SON
I've an impregnable defense. He won't lay a glove on me.
Gosh, Mr. O'Malley! Is Gus all right?
Copyright 1944 Field Publications

Copyright 1944 Field Publications
I believe I've finally imbued Gus with some of my indomitable courage, m'boy. But not having my balance he's become overconfident. And he's underestimating an unscrupulous foe who will make use of an ability to become invisible—
I merely said he won't be able to hit me, O'Malley. I have a PLAN . . .
2·15

What brave strategy have you devised, Gus? . . . To protect you against an unseen antagonist—
It's very simple.
CROCKETT JOHNSON
I shall decline to remove my glasses during the contest.
Gosh.
GUS!

Won't it be kind of a dopey fight, Mr. O'Malley? If Gus can't punch that leprechaun because he won't get visible, and HE can't punch Gus if Gus has his eyeglasses on—
Isn't boxing the art of self-defense, O'Malley?
The spectators will be outraged! We'll be hailed before the boxing commission! Purses held up! It's ridiculous! Absurd!
2-18
Copyright 1944 Field Publications
I can't imagine anything sillier . . . But I'll think of something . . . The crowd will be there to see a FIGHT . . . Between a pair of equally matched contestants—
Ah! I have it!
CROCKETT JOHNSON
If McSnoyd won't make himself visible, I'll wave my magic wand, Gus, and make you invisible too!
Then the crowd won't be able to see ANYTHING!

O'Malley! No! I refuse to be made invisible! Don't do it!
Nothing to it, Gus. Once made myself invisible. Just by—
By accident.
2-17
Anyway, it was quite painless and— But let me refer to this Fairy Godfather's Handy Pocket Guide—"Three waves of a fine Havana magic wand." Thusly—
No!
That's all I'll have to do, Gus, and—Cushlamochree! You're invisible already! Aren't you?
Gosh! Did it work?
CROCKETT JOHNSON
And now, off to the arena! Come on, Gus.
But—
Copyright 1944 Field Publications

No, son, they're not broadcasting a fight this evening between a ghost and a leprechaun . . . And it's way past your bedtime now.
But, gosh—
I may have to go to Washington next week about the dam project. . . . I've got to locate our elusive congressman, J. J. O'Malley, and—
Pop—
Mr. O'Malley, my Fairy Godfather, won't BE in Washington next week. After the fight tonight he must finish the plans of a dam on the brook for the Elves and Gnomes—
Barnaby, go to bed.
CROCKETT JOHNSON
Just rushed over to say goodbye, m'boy. I'm off for Washington at once!
Mr. O'Malley! How did the fight go?

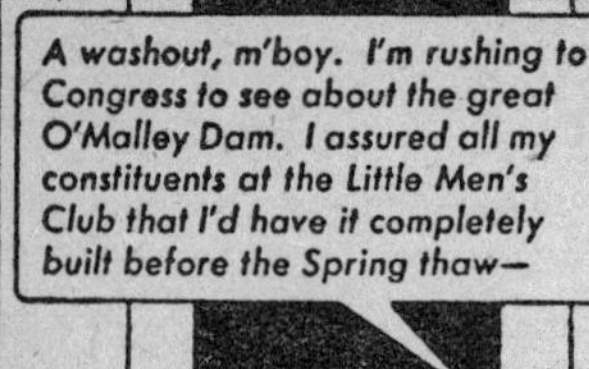
A washout, m'boy. I'm rushing to Congress to see about the great O'Malley Dam. I assured all my constituents at the Little Men's Club that I'd have it completely built before the Spring thaw—

2-19 Copyright 1944 Field Publications
I didn't think it would be a very good fight . . . With both fighters invisible, no wonder it was a—
I'm talking of a literal washout, Barnaby . . . The FIGHT was a thriller!

Had everyone on the edge of his seat! Envisioning the gory struggle taking place in what was seemingly an empty ring! Round after furious round! . . .

CROCKETT JOHNSON
And then, at a most exciting moment in the fourteenth—the Spring THAW set in! We were flooded out!

Gus! Safe and unmarked! Through fourteen rounds of grueling fighting and a flood! . . . But, Gus, how did you regain visibility—
2-21

O'Malley, I never WAS invisible. When you left for the arena, I met my invisible opponent. He was in an aggressively gay mood and insisted that I accompany him to a quaint tavern where—
Won't those elves and gnomes be angry, Mr. O'Malley? When they learn the ring you told them Gus and McSnoyd were boxing in really WAS empty?
Cushlamochree!

Yes . . . But no angrier than they'll be until I'm able to explain about the flood I assured them I'd avert.
Too bad I must flee—I mean FLY, Barnaby—to Washington right away.
CROCKETT JOHNSON

Barnaby, if an irate delegation of elves and gnomes calls here tomorrow, have your mother tell them I've left for Washington. . .
I thought you'd left—
2-22
I can't leave without the plans for the great O'Malley Dam. If Atlas, the Mental Giant, drops by with them, have your mother send him to me in the cellar. . .
I'll tell Mom, Mr. O'Malley.
CROCKETT JOHNSON
Z Z Z Z Z Z Z Z Z Z
Barnaby! Atlas has been here already!
The plans!
Copyright 1944 Field Publications

Mr. O'Malley, Pop's company had a plan made for a big dam. That looks just like—
No. This plan is for the O'Malley Dam.
8-23

All engineers' drawings look alike. To the untutored eye—
Cushlamochree! The important part's left out!
Copyright 1944 Field Publications

The colossal statues on top of the piers!
Come, m'boy. I'll fix that.

CROCKETT JOHNSON
Hold the mirror steady, Barnaby.

It's a letter from Aunt Emma in Washington. Probably offering to put you up while you're there on the negotiations for that dam. . .
Open it and see.
2-24
Well, I'm off, m'boy. I'll have Congress rush through a big appropriation for this dam—
I wish I could go. I'd like to see you passing laws and—

A fine idea. I'll arrange such a trip. At once . . . But, goodbye now, m'boy.
Swell! . . . 'Bye, Mr. O'Malley.
Copyright 1944 Field Publications
Aunt Emma says she'll be delighted to have you, John. . . . And she says can't you arrange to bring Barnaby!
CROCKETT JOHNSON

But I'll be very busy. And do you think Aunt Emma really wants Barnaby on her hands?
She wouldn't invite him if she didn't. . .
2-25
A visit to Washington will be fine for him. He'll see it's a real place. He'll see that Congress is real and decide his imaginary "Mr. O'Malley" can't be a member of it. . .
And he'll stop believing in that pink-winged pixie? Maybe you're right. . . I'll arrange it so that—
Pop! Do you know where I'm going?
Copyright 1944 Field Publications
To Washington, Pop! My Fairy Godfather, Mr. O'Malley, said he would arrange it!
CROCKETT JOHNSON

Ellen, I had six prints of a plan for that proposed dam here the other night. . . One is missing. . . Did you see it?
No. . . I didn't.
Gosh!
2-26
It doesn't matter. I have enough copies. One for our congressman, J. J. O'Malley —if I can LOCATE that chronic absentee. . . And one for—
Mr. O'Malley?
Copyright 1944 Field Publications
Then it's okay. . . Mr. O'Malley, my Fairy Godfather, has his copy of it. He took it to Congress with him. . .
But—GOSH!
CROCKETT JOHNSON
Let's hurry to Washington, Pop! Mr. O'Malley is going to have Congress build it!
THE WRONG DAM!

How many more stops, Pop? Do we go near Alaska? Or Echo Lake? Can the engine go any faster than this? Is Aunt Emma in Congress? Why not, Pop? It's so handy to where she lives . . .
2·29
Barnaby, be quiet for a few minutes. I want to go over these estimates. Try looking out the window for a while.
Okay, Pop.
Here's a picture magazine for the little fellow to look at . . . Help keep him quiet. Heh heh. Talk your ears off, don't they?
Thank you.
. . . This the lad's first visit to Washington? Great place. I know it inside out. Have to, you know. Cotter pins. I'm in the cotter pin line. Say. Heard this one? Friend—happens to be a Senator—told it to me . . .
Copyright 1944 Field Publications
CROCKETT JOHNSON

. . . I know just about everybody in Congress. Personally. You meet people, you know, in the cotter pin business. I drop in now and then for a chat with Speaker Rayburn. Sound man, Rayburn . . .
Yes, indeed . . .
2-29
And Joe Martin—there's a sound man for you. Good old Joseph. He once told me, "Bender," he said—
You must know Congressman Mr. O'Malley—
Congressman O'Malley? Of course. Know him well. VERY well. Sound man, O'Malley.
Gosh.
Copyright 1944 Field Publications
Hey, Pop! Mr. Bender knows Mr. O'Malley, my Fairy Godfather!
Pop! Wake up!
Eh?
CROCKETT JOHNSON

I'm sorry . . . What did you say? About Congressman O'Malley?
Mr. Bender knows him, Pop. He says he's a sound man.
3·1
But he never does anything.
He's never even said anything—
Yes. Sound man. Doesn't fly off in all directions . . .
Pop!
Copyright 1944 Field Publications
Keeps his feet on the ground.
But—
Pop!
CROCKETT JOHNSON

9-2
We're held up here ten minutes. If you want to get off and stretch—
Can I send a telegram?
Pop! I saw—
Send your wire. We'll stroll. I may run into one of my Senator friends. Be a treat for the lad—
Mr. Bender! I see Mr. O'Malley! You know him, you said. Look!
Congressman O'Malley? Of course I know him. But I—
Copyright 1944 Field Publications
JOHNSON
There! At the end of the platform! . . .
MR. O'MALLEY!

Mr. O'Malley. This is Mr. Bender.
He says he knows you very well—
Ee!
Bender? I don't recall having had the pleasure—
3·3
Cushlamochree! Why is he running like that? . . . Over the fence! . . . Oops! On his nose! . . . What ails the man?
Gosh!
Copyright 1944 Field Publications
I've had a bad trip thus far, Barnaby . . . I keep flying off the radio beam. Getting lost—
Can't you stay close to the railroad tracks? . . . They go to Washington.
MAIRZY DOATS
An excellent suggestion . . . And now, if you'll send the candy butcher down with a copy of Harper's Bazaar—
CROCKETT JOHNSON

THERE you are! The train is about to go!
Pop! I met—
Okay, okay. Sit down first and then tell me about it.
But, Pop—
Now . . . What— Say! How did we ever get rid of, I mean, where is what's-his-name? The Man Who Knew O'Malley? . . . He said he was going to Washington—
Mr. Bender?
When we met Mr. O'Malley, my Fairy Godfather, Mr. Bender ran and jumped over a fence and—
Barnaby!
Next station, Washington!
CROCKETT JOHNSON

But, Pop! Mr. O'Malley, my Fairy Godfather, was under this car—
NAIRZY DOATS
Maybe he went right to Congress.
Let's look there—
I didn't know it was so close to the railroad tracks. Let's look—
INFORMATION
This is Union Station! Come along!
TAXIS
It's not Congress? Okay. I'm coming . . .
CROCKETT JOHNSON
Copyright 1944 Field Publications

This cab isn't going our way either.
My Fairy Godfather probably is at Aunt Emma's already, Pop.
9-7
That one is—But it's full . . . How can that imaginary pixie know where we're going, Barnaby? . . .
I told him. . . . To Aunt Emma's . . .
You didn't give him Aunt Emma's address. You don't know it. So—
He'll find it all right, Pop.
CROCKETT JOHNSON
Mmm. I bet he will, too.
Gosh. We should be there. To introduce him to Aunt Emma.
Copyright 1944 Field Publications

Drop me at the Archives Building.
What's that, Pop?
3-8 Copyright 1944 Field Publications
This is the building where the old documents and papers are kept.
The kind Mr. O'Malley and Gus the Ghost get rid of? On the Useless Papers Committee? . . .
Nonsense . . . The building ahead is the Justice Department. And— Barnaby! . . . There are interesting things to see, if you only look!
They throw all the old papers in the river—
Pop! There goes Gus, now! With a stack of them!
CROCKETT JOHNSON

3·8
Hello, John! Hello, Barnaby! So you've finally arrived! . . .
Hello, Aunt Emma.
Did Mr. O'Malley, my Fairy Godfather, get here yet? . . .
Er—I'll explain.
What?
Copyright 1944 Field Publications
Maybe he flew in the window! Which is my room, Aunt Emma?
The little room at the head of the stairs. But—
What is the child talking about?
Aunt Emma, it's rather a long story . . .
CROCKETT JOHNSON

Barnaby and I each have a room to ourselves? In Washington? Why it's—
I'm glad to have you, John . . . George is away on a two-month business trip and with young George in the Navy I'm all alone here. You won't be any trouble . . . Now what's this about Barnaby and a pixie with pink wings named O'Malley?
Hey, Pop! . . . Aunt Emma!
3·10
Gracious! He's terribly upset! He must imagine he sees that creature in his room! Dear me!
POP!
CROCKETT JOHNSON
Mr. O'Malley! He's NOT in my room!
Copyright 1944 Field Publications

3-11
We'll have a busy day seeing the sights tomorrow, son. Say goodnight to Aunt Emma—
But, Mr. O'Malley, my Fairy Godfather, said he'd be here—

Somebody's at the window! It's him! It's Mr. O'Malley!
TAP!
TAP!
TAP!
Copyright 1944 Field Publications

The invisible leprechaun!
Tell the Honorable J. J. O'Malley three leryal constituents yoin for a audience with his great and august poisonage . . .
CROCKETT JOHNSON

THREE invisible leprechauns!
Where IS the joik?
Us three was appernted as a delegation.
Yerse.

Pop! There are leprechauns in my room! They're looking for Mr. O'Malley! A delegation!
Nonsense!
3-13
You've been dreaming again, son. Anyway, they're not here now . . .
I guess they've gone. Okay, I'll go back to bed. Goodnight, Pop.
If Congressman Mr. O'Malley, my Fairy Godfather, was here he'd show those leprechauns—
Yes, indeed, Barnaby . . .
Copyright 1944 Field Publications
CROCKETT JOHNSON
My actions cannot be influenced by pressure groups! . . . Er, are you sure they've gone? . . .
Mr. O'Malley!

3-14
I thought maybe you had trouble getting here. You didn't know what street Aunt Emma's house is on or what her name is or—
I procured this excellent tourist's map, m'boy. Has everything on it. Clearly marked . . . Capitol . . . White House . . . Smithsonian Institute . . . Aunt Emma's house . . . Washington Monument . . . Library of Congress . . .
No. I'm late arriving because I went first to the Archives Building to see Gus and then to Congress to rally support for the O'Malley Dam. I have the old steamroller oiled up!
CROCKETT JOHNSON
Backing for the measure has increased a hundred percent! Representative Rumpelstilskin has promised to vote with me. We have a solid block of two—
Rumpelstilskin?

Representative Rumpelstilskin, the silver-tongued obstructionist, isn't the irrational creature he seems to be. To win his support one must understand him. Ignore political and economic motives and explore the psychological!
Oh.
I ran into the little fellow in the Congressional washroom. Wishing to be friendly, I asked him what he was marking on the walls. He snarled that he was figuring how to raise the poll tax to keep pace with the cost of living. Then he slugged me!
Gosh.
CROCKETT JOHNSON
It was difficult winning his support sitting on his chest. . . Then, too, he had the idea I was a Mr. Pearson, a Baptist who had changed his name from Winchell. He also decried me as a meddling foreigner!
Are you a foreigner?
Well, yes. I came over with a shipload of refugees on a tub called The Màyflower. By an error, the Travel Bureau sent me—But that's another story. Where was I? Oh, yes. Winning Rumpelstilskin's friendship . . .
Copyright 1944 Field Publications

Representative Rumpelstilskin's incoherent shrieks about states' rights subsided and he passed from his manic period into one of depression. This mood makes analysis difficult But I delved to the bottom of his neurosis . . .
What did you find?
3-16
The poll tax! Rumpelstilskin is elected by only 2½ percent of the people in his districts. Other congressmen get eleven times his vote. Representing a minority group, he feels he doesn't amount to very much.
He's offensive because he's on the defensive. Inferiority. I saw we'd have to strike right at the root of the trouble to bring old Rump back to his real sweet self. "My friend," I assured him, "We'll get rid of that poll tax."
Copyright 1944 Field Publications
CROCKETT JOHNSON
What did he say to that, Mr. O'Malley?
I couldn't make it out. He's incoherent in his manic mood.

Mentioning the poll tax wasn't the way to win Rumpelstilskin's cooperation I decided, so I set about finding another approach. Just then Gus arrived with the plans for the O'Malley Dam. I'd left them behind inadvertently.
Gus is a very spic and span ghost in the new sheets I procured for him. Rump was fascinated by Gus's lack of pigmentation, complete except for the word "Statler" in red on his hem. Rump's eyes lit up!
CROCKETT JOHNSON
"The Perfect Aryan!" he yelled. He at once agreed to support our dam if Gus would do him the honor of voting for him on election day. This will cost Gus $42 in back taxes but, all in all, everything ended happily.
Later I learned we needn't have gone to all that trouble. Rump votes for all dams anyway. He likes the sound of the word . . . I must be off now, m'boy. Got to rally up vote number three . . .

Well, Barnaby. All set to visit the office of Congressman O'Malley?
He was here last night, Pop. And—
Copyright 1944 Field Publications
If we find him in, and he's a real man, you'll admit this pink-winged pixie of yours is all a dream, won't you, son?
But—
His office isn't here, Pop. He—
We'll see . . .
CROCKETT JOHNSON
Congressman O'Malley? . . . Room 32958.
Pop! There must be a mistake!

This is Congressman O'Malley's floor, Barnaby. Watch your step.
But—
3·20
Copyright 1944 Field Publications

FLOOR DIRECTORY
I'm sure he's not here, Pop.

You and your old man soiching for O'Malley too, kid? He ain't here.
Gosh!
The joik is averding us.
Yerse!

His office is this way. Didn't I hear you talking to someone?
Three leprechauns. They couldn't find Mr. O'Malley either.
CROCKETT JOHNSON

Barnaby, the officer said Congressman O'Malley is on this floor. The directory says so. If he's not in, a secretary will be in his office. So—
Mr. O'Malley hasn't got an office, Pop... Gus the Ghost is his secretary. And they both live over at the old papers building.
3-21
Copyright 1944 Field Publications

CROCKETT JOHNSON
You mean the Archives Building? Nonsense... There's his office. At the end of the hall...
Huh?

Representative
J.J.O'MALLEY

Just look at the mail! The door's locked, of course.
Representative
J. J. O'MALLEY
What's in that, Pop?
3·22

The big box? Books or something. From Congressman Bloom. . . . This whole thing is—It's unbelievable!

CROCKETT JOHNSON
When people learn about Congressman O'Malley and this office he's never even set foot in! . . .
But when MR. O'MALLEY learns about this office!
Representative
J. J. O'MALLEY
Copyright 1944 Field Publications

So we spent the rest of the day sightseeing. . . I'll see what I can do about getting that dam approved on my own. I can't waste any more time hunting for Congressman O'Malley. . . Nobody knows him. We've looked every place for him and—
We didn't look EVERY place, Aunt Emma
You ought to run along to bed, Barnaby.
O'Malley certainly knows how to avoid his constituents. . .
CROCKETT JOHNSON
O'Malley is always eager to welcome one of his beloved constituents. . . Whether from the great palaces or from the slums of our beautiful 17th Congressional District—
Noitz.
Cut the erl, O'Malley.
Yerse.
Copyright 1944 Field Publications

You don't know what it means to a congressman in this big cold city of Washington! A voice from home! A familiar face! What do you boys want?
The three invisible leprechauns! They found Mr. O'Malley!
Where's that dam, O'Malley? For our moimuring brook?
We want soivice!
Yerse!
Copyright 1944 Field Publications
The dam for the brook? Friends, I can report great progress! I'm calling a caucus on the subject of the Great O'Malley Dam. And Representative Rumpelstilskin and I will discuss it at length—
No more voibiage! Get us that dam!
Or else!
Yerse!
And when you return home, tell my many dear friends—
We ain't retoining. Without that dam.
Nope!
Yerse!
CROCKETT JOHNSON

Those leprechauns! Like all constituents! Expect their congressman to achieve the impossible! Cushlamochree!
Pop is looking for you, Mr. O'Malley.
3-25
I'll be delighted to see him, m'boy. Is he downstairs now? Fine! Be a pleasure to have a quiet chat with somebody who doesn't want something. We'll discuss tennis—Or, say! Does your dad play chess?
But—
Pop wants you to get Congress to build a dam, Mr. O'Malley—
Another dam? Cushlamochree!
Copyright 1944 Field Publications
I can't stay. I've got to prepare an agenda for the big caucus meeting with Representative Rumpelstilskin!
CROCKETT JOHNSON

Pop, Congressman Mr. O'Malley, my Fairy Godfather, is going to get that dam built for you . . . He's getting one just like it for the elves in the woods . . .
So he says he can have Congress order two at the same time and save money. He's economizing . . .
Run up and wash before dinner, son.
Representative Rumpelstilskin promised Mr. O'Malley his vote. . . . By now he's probably got ALL the congressmen persuaded . . .
Fine . . . I'll bank on that, Barnaby.
Copyright 1944 Field Publications
CROCKETT JOHNSON
Mr. O'Malley! Did you persuade everybody—
Catastrophe, m'boy! Rumpelstilskin has changed his mind!

Representative Rumpelstilskin withdrew his support from the Great O'Malley Dam bill! And why? . . . Merely because I don't appreciate his JOKES! . . . Can you imagine such sensitivity?
He tells jokes?
Stuff his gagman clips from old copies of Der Stürmer . . . Rump prides himself on his delivery. It goes big in Congress . . . But, as I told him, comedy standards differ. And mine are the severe ones of an old Minsky devotee.
I tried to explain cultural lags and things. It was no use . . . All is lost, Barnaby.
Can you stay to dinner, Mr. O'Malley? . . . Aunt Emma will be glad to—
I can't be bothered with the thought of FOOD, m'boy! In this serious political crisis!
Gosh! It MUST be serious!
CROCKETT JOHNSON

The Great O'Malley Dam may never be built, Barnaby. And my political future hangs in the balance. What worries . . . Thanks for your invitation to dinner . . . But I've no appetite.
Gosh.
3-29
Besides, I've already dined. At the home of an old Washington family on Pennsylvania Avenue. In their lovely white mansion—
What's the family's name, Mr. O'Malley?
One member of the household is named Fala. He's a Scottish Terrier . . . None of the others wandered into the pantry, so—
BARNABY
Dinner's ready.
Copyright 1944 Field Publications
Yes. Run along and enjoy your repast, m'boy. Leave your old Fairy Godfather with his worries . . . Mmmm.
ZZZZZZ.
CROCKETT JOHNSON

Mr. O'Malley! I know how you can get Congress to build that dam for you!
I've thought of a way, too, Barnaby. What's your idea?

Wave your magic wand!
Hmmm . . . No.

What is it?
Such a method would be attacked by certain elements as undemocratic . . . And by others as unconstitutional. No. I've a better plan. I'll get it underway at once!

No time to lose, m'boy . . . The Great O'Malley Dam will be passed by Congress tomorrow!
But, how—
CROCKETT JOHNSON

I've spent a week going from office to office explaining how badly our city needs that power dam. I've gotten no place! . . . If we had a congressman who—
RING RING
The doorbell.
3-31
Mr. O'Malley, my Fairy Godfather, said Congress would pass on his bill for a dam today, Pop. And—
A telegram . . . For you, John.
"Congratulations to you and to Congressman O'Malley . . . Never dreamed Congress would approve our dam so soon" . . . It's from my boss! What is this, Aunt Emma? . . .
Copyright 1944 Field Publications
Of course! It's an April Fools' gag of some kind. It must be—
No, it isn't, Pop. Congress passed it all right . . .
CROCKETT JOHNSON

Oh, hello, dear . . . Yes . . . Barnaby and I may as well come home. I've done everything I can do on the power dam. And it wasn't much. . . . What? . . . Who's being modest?
. . . What's that about an April Fool joke? . . . But Mr. Bronson DID send that telegram of congratulation . . . WHY? Why did he SEND it? . . . John. Have you and that Congressman O'Malley been celebrating? . . .
Of course it's in the local papers . . . A large double headline all across the page . . . Shall I read it?
Yes . . . Slowly.
Rep. J. J. O'Malley Wins Congressional Approval of Local Dam Project! . . .
John? Are you there?
CROCKETT JOHNSON

43
Mr. O'Malley—
Just in time, m'boy. . . I am explaining to my three invisible constituents here how I maneuvered the Great O'Malley Dam through Congress. . . Like all great strategists, I conceived a simple plan, the success of which depended on perfect timing—
Never mind the dissoitation, pal.
Tell us how you done it.
Yerse.
Copyright 1944 Field Publications

I appended the proposed drawings, description, estimates—all of which Atlas had worked out—in the form of a Rider. . .to a Motion to Adjourn!
Those plans—
Impossible! . . . Absoid!
A motion to adjoin is voibal!
Yerse!

Impossible? Remember my coup was perfectly TIMED! . . . Friday! . . . 3 p.m.! NOTHING's impossible for a Congress eager to get away for the weekend!
But—
CROCKETT JOHNSON

Barnaby!... All that noise! What was it?
Those three invisible leprechauns were cheering because Mr. O'Malley, my Fairy Godfather, got Congress to pass the bill for that dam. Mr. O'Malley looked kind of funny riding on their shoulders and—

Don't tell stories like that, son... That loud crash! What was it?
The loud crash?... When I told them Mr. O'Malley passed the wrong dam...

CROCKETT JOHNSON
The invisible leprechauns DROPPED Mr. O'Malley...
Barnaby!

Thanks for everything.
It was lovely having you both, John. . . I'm sorry to have you go. . . I wish I could say as much for your imaginary pixie friend, Barnaby. . . Say. You ARE taking that Fairy Godfather with you?
Mr. O'Malley?
4-5

I wish we COULD leave him behind, Aunt Emma. But Barnaby always insists on taking him with him—
I'm glad of that—
No—

CROCKETT JOHNSON
Mr. O'Malley has to get Congress to pass another bill, Aunt Emma. . . He's staying here with YOU.

4·6
CROCKETT JOHNSON
Pop, this ride home is kind of dull, isn't it?
Delightfully dull, Barnaby.

4-7
Hello.
Hello, Mom.
Hello!
Copyright 1944 Field Publications
Tell me all about it! How you and Congressman O'Malley got Congress to approve the dam.
You may not believe this. . . I didn't have a THING to do with it—
Mom—
Mr. O'Malley, my Fairy Godfather, got it passed, Mom. By mistake—
Hush, Barnaby. John, tell me—
For all I know, Ellen, Barnaby's explanation is as good as any—
Oh, John. But of course, if it's a business secret—
But—
CROCKETT JOHNSON

Well, however Congressman O'Malley managed to do it, getting that power dam approved has made him a hero in this town. . . This laudatory editorial points out how he's grown in stature—
Mr. O'Malley, my Fairy Godfather? Gosh! How much has he grown?. . .
Barnaby. It's your bedtime.
4-8
Copyright 1944 Field Publications
Do you think Mr. O'Malley has grown too big to get through my window, Mom?
Stop being silly, son. Goodnight.
CROCKETT JOHNSON
Mr. O'Malley! . . . You haven't grown at all!
Eh?

This editorial refers to my growth in POLITICAL stature, m'boy . . . A figure of speech—
Oh. I thought you grew up. Or got fatter.
Copyright 1944 Field Publications
4 10
Did you also get Congress to pass the dam the Elves want? For the brook in the woods?
". . . grown in the public eye . . ." Eh? What did you say?
. . . The original site of the Great O'Malley Dam? They don't need a dam there any more, Barnaby. The beavers came back . . . SAY!
What?
CROCKETT JOHNSON
. . . The symbolic statues of me for the river dam! . . . Now that I've grown in stature, m'boy! . . .
. . . Those colossal twin figures are too small!

Are you going to order bigger statues of you for the power dam than you put in the plans?
Naturally, m'boy . . . The papers say I've grown in stature . . .
4-11
Dimensions of both colossal figures must be increased by the exact amount I've grown.
How much have you grown, Mr. O'Malley?
Copyright 1944 Field Publications
Astronomically! A precise calculation is a gigantic task. Only a Mental Giant can cope with the problem.
Atlas?
CROCKETT JOHNSON
Yes. Atlas, the Mental Giant!
Fe, fie, ho, hum.

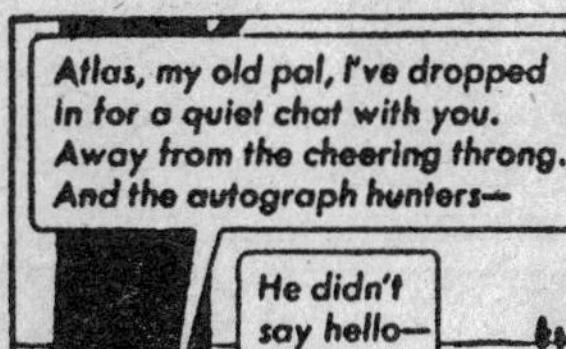
Atlas, my old pal, I've dropped in for a quiet chat with you. Away from the cheering throng. And the autograph hunters—

He didn't say hello—
4 12

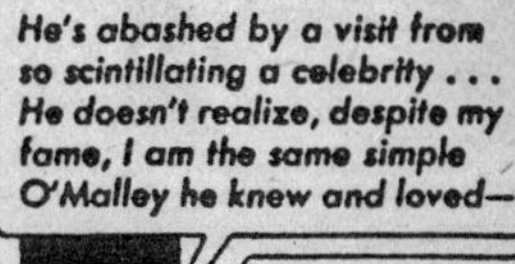
He's abashed by a visit from so scintillating a celebrity . . . He doesn't realize, despite my fame, I am the same simple O'Malley he knew and loved—

He's walking away.
Copyright 1944 Field Publications

Atlas, as you are aware, the one name today on everyone's lips is "Congressman O'Malley." I daresay it will soon be "Senator O'Malley!" . . . And, if the Chicago conventions heed the will of the people, who knows—But what I came for is—

CROCKETT JOHNSON
Mr. O'Malley. Atlas doesn't remember you.
Cushlamochree!

This is humiliating! A celebrated personage! My name a household word! . . . And this absent-minded Mental Giant has to figure out who I am with his memory aid! . . .
I still think it would be easier for Atlas to remember names instead of those formulas he has to work out on his slide rule, Mr. O'Malley. . . . And I have to go home soon . . .
$S\left(O!+\frac{1}{3}\frac{dM^3}{dM}\right)=$
4·13
Copyright 1944 Field Publications
But he makes no embarrassing mistakes in identity this way . . . Mathematics don't lie, you know. . . .Ah . . . He has the solution! Now watch him greet me effusively!
SI+MMS
Addison SIMMS! And how is everything in Seattle, Mr. Simms! . . .

O'Malley! I didn't recognize you. You've changed. You had on earmuffs last time. And I—
They're my winter garb. December 21 to March 21. . . . But I HAVE changed.
4-14

I've increased in political stature, Atlas . . . And I've come to you to find out exactly how much. So I'll know how much bigger I must make the colossal bronze figures of me on the Great O'Malley Dam.

It will take only a few hours to calculate on your slide rule how I have grown in the Public Eye . . .
I have to go home now . . .

CROCKETT JOHNSON
Which eye, O'Malley? Right eye? . . . Or left—

Pop, Mr. O'Malley, my Fairy Godfather, and a friend of his, Atlas the Mental Giant, are figuring how much bigger to make the statues of Mr. O'Malley—

Quiet, Barnaby . . . I'm talking to the chief engineer on the big power dam project . . .

CROCKETT JOHNSON

The WPB has approved all of our specifications? . . . Except WHAT? . . . Colossal bronze statues?. . . Angels! Or winged victory symbols! . . . But our plans didn't call for statues! . . .

Maybe the architects know what the WPB is talking about. . .But I—
I know, Pop—
BARNABY! QUIET!

Hush, m'boy... Atlas the Mental Giant is calculating my political growth from the time I was prevailed upon to enter public office. We'll soon know how big to make those colossal statues of me so they will adequately reflect my increased stature.
You're still growing, O'Malley. According to today's editorials.
But, Mr. O'Malley—
4-17

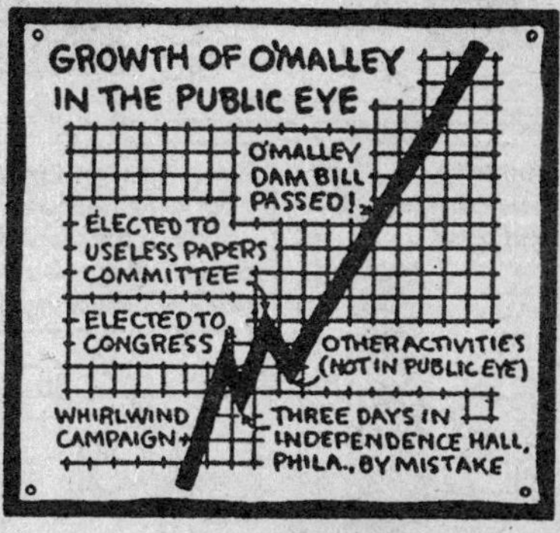
GROWTH OF O'MALLEY IN THE PUBLIC EYE
O'MALLEY DAM BILL PASSED!
ELECTED TO USELESS PAPERS COMMITTEE
ELECTED TO CONGRESS
OTHER ACTIVITIES (NOT IN PUBLIC EYE)
WHIRLWIND CAMPAIGN
THREE DAYS IN INDEPENDENCE HALL, PHILA., BY MISTAKE

You realize, O'Malley, we can't tell how large those bronze statues of you must be until you STOP growing.
Cushlamochree!

Pop says the War Production Board won't let them put two thirty-ton bronze statues of you on the city's new power dam, Mr. O'Malley. Because—
Ah, yes. . . The WPB realizes that thirty-ton monuments are far too small. But I'm constantly growing in the public eye, Barnaby. And by next week, who knows, NINETY-ton statues may also be inadequate. . .
4-18
Copyright 1944 Field Publications
Have your dad tell the WPB we're sorry, but we can't use metal at all. . .
Yes. There's a shortage—
The colossal twin statues of your Fairy Godfather which will grace the piers of the Great O'Malley Dam will be made of pneumatic RUBBER!
CROCKETT JOHNSON

Inflated rubber statues of me will be an enormous success, m'boy. As my popularity increases, enthusiastic constituents will be permitted to aid in making the statues bigger. . . At a nominal charge, say, a dime a blow—
Who gets the dimes?
4-19

The dimes? They'll all go into the coffers of the organization I shall set up and administer personally—
What's that, Mr. O'Malley?

The J. J. O'Malley Self-Perpetuating Vulcanizing Fund.

Is it true what I hoid, O'Malley? You're going to get them to build statues of you out of rubber?
The invisible leprechaun!
Yes. . . So they can be blown up to heroic proportions to keep pace exactly with my steadily growing importance. How does the idea strike you, McSnoyd?
4-20

CROCKETT JOHNSON
A very praiseworthy Idear! They'll be poifectly realistic too, them windbag statues—
Ah! . . . Good luck!
What are you picking up? . . .

And another voitue of them rubber statues of you, pal, is—
McSNOYD! . . . Stop whetting that PIN!

No, Barnaby, I rather doubt if the War Production Board will let that imaginary Fairy Godfather of yours have enough rubber to build big statues of himself. . .
But you're not sure. . .
4 21
I wonder what the WPB would say to a request for a priority so that a pink-winged pixie can—
I'm finding out, Pop. . .
CROCKETT JOHNSON
I want to ask the WPB— Yes. In Washington—if Mr. O'Malley— Hello. . .
Longah Distance. . . Hello. . . . Hold the Tion puleez. . .
A lion? Gosh. . .

Pop doesn't think you ought to bother the WPB for rubber for those statues of you now, Mr. O'Malley. The shortage—
I've decided that too, m'boy. . . Because as I continue to grow in stature, I'll achieve NATIONAL prominence. . . And every town and hamlet will want an O'Malley pneumatic monument of its own. . . The demand will be too great.
4-22
So, intriguing as the thought is of a colossal statue of your Fairy Godfather in every park and market place, Barnaby, we must forget it. . . Temporarily. . .
The idea is being written up, however, by a talented advertising writer I keep supplied with new slants on the Post-War World.

I'm convinced that if we go on humoring Barnaby, we'll never shake his belief in that little man with pink wings he dreams about. We've got to REASON him out of this ridiculous idea. Once and for all!
Well, maybe you can do it.
4 24

CROCKETT JOHNSON
We'll demolish this imaginary pixie by drawing a clear line in the boy's mind between logical scientific fact and childish superstitious nonsense.
I'll call Barnaby. You talk to him.
Copyright 1944 Field Publications

A burning feeling in my ear, Barnaby. Supposed to mean someone's talking about me. . . Of course, that's nothing but childish superstitious nonsense . . .

. . . And you see why this little pixie can't really exist, don't you? . . . Look at it another way—
But, gosh, Pop—
4 25

Take other children. Take your little friend, Jane Schultz. Has she a "Fairy Godfather"? No—
No.

That's why Mr. O'Malley, my Fairy Godfather, feels kind of sorry for her. He drops over there now and then to cheer her up. But she—
Barnaby.
CROCKETT JOHNSON

Look. . . This trick is amazing. Take a card, Jane. Any card—
But I want to read my new funny book
CAPTAIN Bloodbath

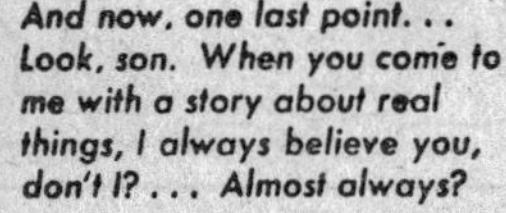
And now, one last point. . .
Look, son. When you come to me with a story about real things, I always believe you, don't I? . . . Almost always?

Sure, Pop.
4·26

But when you tell me about a cigar-smoking pixie with pink wings! I can't believe THAT. Any more than I could believe that dog can TALK.
But, Pop—

Now run along and play, son. . .
I've got a phone call to make. . .

CROCKETT JOHNSON
I guess he doesn't know about me, does he? About your mother not allowing me to sit on this couch.
Copyright 1944 Field Publications

Jane has persuaded me to do my amazing card trick, m'boy. . . . Remember your card, Jane. Now I shuffle the deck. And—
Mr. O'Malley—
CAPTAIN Bloodbath
4·27

And here's the card you picked! Ace of Hearts!
No. King of Clubs.
Look, Barnaby! . . . She's astounded!
CAPTAIN Bloodbath

CROCKETT JOHNSON
Mr. O'Malley! Pop says you can't possibly exist!
Take a card, m'boy. Any card—WHAT? I don't exist? Me?
CAPTAIN Bloodbath

I'm sure I can convince him I do exist. With my command of logic. . . Is your father home now? Fine! . . . Your old Fairy Godfather's ever eager for a good metaphysical argument!
CAPTAIN Bloodbath
Copyright 1944 Field Publications

What ever made your dad say such a thing? . . . I don't exist! Me! Of all people!
Pop has never seen you. He says I only imagine you're real.
Copyright 1944 Field Publications 4-28
Shades of Bishop Berkeley! I'll prove to him by my sound logic that his position is untenable. Then I'll marshal an array of convincing facts and figures—
Pop's in the living room now. . . . Aren't you going right in to argue with him, Mr. O'Malley?
I must leave no shadow of doubt in his mind. . .
CROCKETT JOHNSON
Suppose I brush up for an hour or so on the data I'll use in my argument.
Where does your dad keep his library card?

That public library! . . . Every research work on us pixies is a libelous lie! . . . We're called "imaginary creatures in folk superstition"! Cushlamochree!
4-29
I found a few undocumented and dilettantish reports with an occasional bit of truth in them. But on FICTION shelves! No wonder your dad is prone to doubt my very existence!
I think if you just bust in on Pop and say you really exist—
My word against all those charlatans he accepts as scientific authorities? . . . No.
CROCKETT JOHNSON
He'd never believe me, Barnaby...
I guess maybe he wouldn't, Mr. O'Malley.

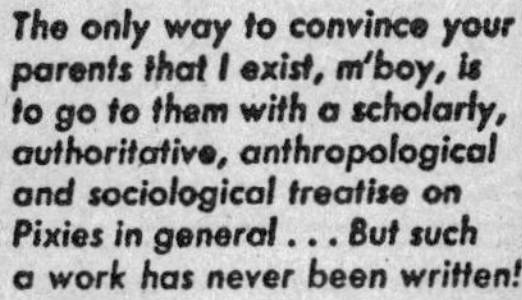
The only way to convince your parents that I exist, m'boy, is to go to them with a scholarly, authoritative, anthropological and sociological treatise on Pixies in general . . . But such a work has never been written!

Gosh.
5-1

The custodians of the Library of Congress reading room and the athenaeum of the Elves, Leprechauns, Gnomes and Little Men's Chowder and Marching Society both agreed that it is indeed a fine state of affairs!

They apologetically referred me to Chaucer, Spencer, Shakespeare, Doyle, Stephens and others—who, as I pointed out, had no academic standing and whose conflicting data would carry no weight with your scientifically-minded dad . . .
Then you can't prove to Pop—
Copyright 1944 Field Publications

I intend to bring your father incontrovertible truth, m'boy. . . . An exhaustive, documented work on the subject of Pixies. . . . I shall write it MYSELF!
CROCKETT JOHNSON

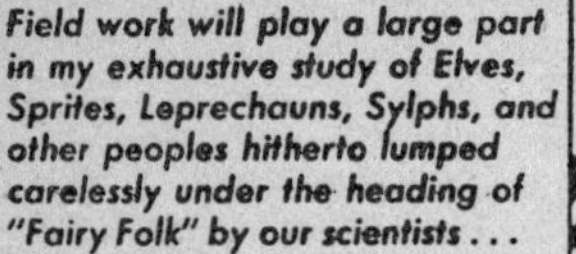

Field work will play a large part in my exhaustive study of Elves, Sprites, Leprechauns, Sylphs, and other peoples hitherto lumped carelessly under the heading of "Fairy Folk" by our scientists . . .
5-2

I'll also settle the etymological controversy on the generic name "Fairy" itself. There's an absurd belief that it's related to the Persian "Peri," meaning "fallen one!" Instead of the much more apt Latin "Fatum," or "destiny". . .
CROCKETT JOHNSON

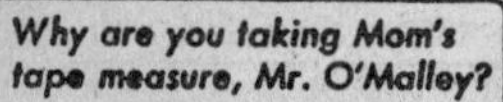

Why are you taking Mom's tape measure, Mr. O'Malley?
Thousands of pages of my work must be devoted to Physical Anthropological Data.

We must measure the craniums and shinbones of all the Little Folk in the woods . . . Yes, Scienc is a tedious taskmaster! . . . Let's be off, m'boy, on our field trip.
Copyright 1944 Field Publications

Barnaby, I think I'll give my great research work a short, modest title . . . Just "PIXIES."
That's quite short.
5-3
Then for a subtitle: "A Complete and Authoritative Sociological and Anthropological Study, Based on Exhaustive Field Work, of All Existing Varieties; Their Physical Characteristics; Their Economic Base and Cultural Superstructure;
Copyright 1944 Field Publications
"With Analytical Conclusions on Their Origins and Future Development; In 36 Volumes; By Doctor J. J. O'Malley . . ."
Doctor?
CROCKETT JOHNSON
Yes. I'll be showered with degrees when the news of this project of mine reaches academic circles—
There, Barnaby! Our first subject! . . . That invisible Leprechaun!

Launcelot McSnoyd! Fine! I'll begin my exhaustive study of all varieties of Pixies with you Leprechauns! A few questions, McSnoyd, which I'll present in the strict methodological manner we anthropologists require—
What have you cooked up now, O'Malley? In that old berlerhead?. . .
That invisible Leprechaun! He called you a Boilerhead, Mr. O'Malley—
CROCKETT JOHNSON
5·4

No insults, McSnoyd. Must be no antagonism between scientist and subject, you know. It's a cardinal rule in anthropological field work—
A card— Say! . . . Thanks for reminding me.
Copyright 1944 Field Publications

There. That's better. I'm glad you're cooperating . . . And now—
Mr. O'Malley. He went that way . . .
I have a oljent apperntment. . .

CROCKETT JOHNSON
McSnoyd, I must have all the data on you Leprechauns. In minute detail. Nothing can dissuade me from my exacting scientific task . . . We can't leave anything to chance, you know, in the anthropology game . . .
How can you measure his head, Mr. O'Malley? . . . If he's invisible? . . .
Noitz. I'm late now . . .
Yes. And I'll have to ask you to make yourself visible. We must measure you, McSnoyd, for your cephalic index . . .
I don't want to poichase nothing, pal.
Least of all a cephalic index. Also I am due in the back room of the Chowder and Marching Club. A little game of chance—
A game of chance?

The Leprechaun said that—er—a game of chance was in progress in the back room of the Elves, Leprechauns, Gnomes and Little Men's Chowder and Marching Society, Barnaby, did he not? . . .
Yes.
5·8

Are you going there too, Mr. O'Malley? . . . Instead of getting that science data on Leprechauns for the book you're writing?
Yes, I'm going there, m'boy . . . To continue my research. Gambling practises give an anthropologist great insight into the culture of a people . . . Of course, the game itself is to me a boring affair . . .

CROCKETT JOHNSON
But perhaps I can induce them this time to make aces and deuces wild . . .
Copyright 1944 Field Publications